Alex Pettes
April 2017

Advance praise for **EVERYONE'S AN ARTIST**

"Fresh, funny and practical, *Everyone's an Artist* shows how the habits of successful artists can help anyone become smarter, faster and better."

—**CHARLES DUHIGG**, *New York Times*–bestselling author of *Smarter Faster Better* and *The Power of Habit*

"Never has there been a book so primed for the business world that we all live in. Worried about your job? Thinking about when the robots are going to take your work too? Get creative! Don't just think like an artist. Be an artist. You are one. It's not just a smart title for a great book, either. This is your road map. Buy this book and embrace it!"

—**MITCH JOEL**, author of *Six Pixels of Separation* and *Ctrl Alt Delete*

"The first book that documents the importance and significance of art and the artist in the science of success. Buy it, read it and paint your own masterpiece."

—**JEFFREY GITOMER**, author of *Little Red Book of Selling*

"Society loves the What (was delivered) and has a growing appreciation for the How (it was delivered). Yet the secret behind happiness is the underappreciated Why, which is the gateway to being an artist. I'm delighted that Ron, Scott and Christopher have an engaging road map for anyone who wants success plus happiness!"

—AVINASH KAUSHIK, author of *Web Analytics 2.0*

"If you have ever looked for a way to let your creative self out of your head and into your life, this book is your road map. Creativity and an artist's mindset make everything in our lives more colourful, more interesting and more productive. In *Everyone's An Artist*, the authors give you all the tools to be more than you thought you could be in every aspect of your life. You will enjoy the easy read and you will benefit from its excellent advice. Buy it, read it and be an artist again!"

—CHESTER ELTON, *New York Times*–bestselling co-author of *The Carrot Principle*, *All In* and *What Motivates Me*

"I always considered artists to be the weird stepchild of the creativity world. I was wrong! This book makes a compelling case for why anyone can—and must—be an artist as a means of enhancing creativity. Treat yourself to this book. It is a work of art!"

—STEPHEN M. SHAPIRO, author of *Best Practices Are Stupid*

EVERYONE'S AN ARTIST

EVERYONE'S AN ARTIST

How Creativity Gives You the Edge in Everything You Do

RON TITE
SCOTT KAVANAGH
CHRISTOPHER NOVAIS

Collins

Everyone's an Artist
Copyright © 2016 by Ron Tite and The Art Of Productions Inc.
All rights reserved.

Published by Collins, an imprint of HarperCollins Publishers Ltd

First edition

HarperCollins books may be purchased for educational, business,
or sales promotional use through our Special Markets Department.

HarperCollins Publishers Ltd
2 Bloor Street East 20th Floor
Toronto, Ontario, Canada
M4W 1A8

harpercollins.ca

Library and Archives Canada Cataloguing in Publication
information is available upon request.

ISBN 978-1-44342-630-5

Printed and bound in the United States of America
RRD 9 8 7 6 5 4 3 2 1

This book is dedicated to all the free spirits who choose to express themselves.

CONTENTS

INTRODUCTION

When Dr. John Semple, chief surgeon at Toronto's Women's College Hospital, faces a patient with a baffling health problem or tackles a complicated medical situation, he often finds himself grateful for one aspect of his training. That training, however, didn't happen during his courses at medical school or during his many long shifts of residency. No, it's not anything that hours of watching *Grey's Anatomy* might lead you to suspect. What Dr. Semple is especially happy to have in his medical tool belt are his years of painting, sculpting and drawing.

Long before Dr. Semple headed to medical school, he attended the Ontario College of Art (known today as OCAD University). After three years there, he completed an undergraduate degree in medical illustration at the

University of Toronto. It's those years as an artist that he finds of so much value in his present work as a doctor, researcher and medical administrator.

Staring at a blank canvas (which is what all artists do either literally or metaphorically when they set out to create their work) trained Dr. Semple's mind in a way no amount of textbook study or operating room drama could. "It's the way you think as an artist that's so important," Dr. Semple told the *Globe and Mail* in a June 2012 profile. "Thinking as an artist means connecting the dots that aren't next to each other. . . . From a research point of view, that can mean looking at things in ways people haven't looked at before." He credits this mental flexibility with helping him make breakthroughs in his research on the effects of hypoxia on high-altitude mountain climbers and with allowing him to develop a mobile health project that lets patients use a smartphone app to reduce hospital visits after surgery. As he told us when we talked with him about his work, "People tend to be so siloed; we tend to focus on only one thing. But I think it's the overlap areas, the areas between those silos that is so interesting. Creativity lives in those areas."

RECENTLY THERE HAS BEEN a spate of articles, books and reports about artists or people with degrees in the liberal arts who are doing other things for a living. Or put another way, articles about highly successful people in the worlds of business, technology and health who have training in the arts and the humanities. *Forbes* magazine published a much reposted article entitled "That 'Useless' Arts Degree Has Become Tech's Hottest Ticket," which discussed the fact that the tech world is hiring just as many people with arts backgrounds as those with tech training. *Time* ran an article about ten CEOs of wildly successful companies, like Starbucks, Hewlett-Packard and Avon, who have liberal arts degrees. The *Globe and Mail* recently wrote a profile of a National Ballet of Canada dancer turned physiatrist, and the article about Dr. Semple, the visual arts major who became a surgeon. And much has been made of the fact that visionary tech designer and developer Steve Jobs took a creative writing course and studied calligraphy in his pre-Apple days (which he talked about extensively in his now famous Stanford University convocation address).

So, what's going on here? Is everyone just tickled by the idea that our high school guidance counsellors screwed up, that despite their well-meaning advice, we *can* build a successful career without an undergraduate degree in business or engineering?

Yes, there are a good number of us who are happy that our guidance counsellors were wrong—about university courses, about career choices, about our chances of ending up in jail. But it's more than that. Consider the way most of us live our lives. We are told to get off our Fisher-Price booster seats and head to kindergarten. So we do. And we obediently continue on that pint-sized treadmill, through grade school and summer camps, high school and sports teams. As we move toward adulthood, we begin to think about employment—and how to get there. We take courses and degrees. We start at some entry-level position. We embrace the work culture of wherever we end up. And while we follow the rules of the workplace, we also follow the expectations of society—finding a partner, buying a house, having kids, signing up for a seldom-used gym membership. Although that time-honoured routine is practical and effective, it puts many of us in a rut.

Before we know it, we're at some meeting being asked to create a new approach for a business venture, and inspiration is as hard to find as someone who admits to being a Nickelback fan. Or we are faced with a tricky social situation, and the only solution we can come up with is to binge-watch the Food Network and hope it goes away. Or maybe our problem is even greater. Maybe we recognize the life we want to live or an accomplishment we want to achieve, but just can't see a way to make it happen.

What all of the articles about "arts success stories" are pointing to is that the conventional wisdom about how to succeed, how to achieve our goals, is not looking all that wise these days. In our highly competitive, overpopulated world, we are beginning to notice that it's rarely the traditionalists who are breaking away from the pack, doing innovative things, changing the world, bettering lives and being truly successful in their fields. (Consider this: one-third of Fortune 500 CEOs have arts degrees!)

Sometimes training and disciplines that seem impractical or abstract or—God forbid—fun are intensely useful. Many people in business, science and technology are recognizing that employees with backgrounds in the humanities, especially in English and philosophy, have been trained to think analytically, to process information, to find meaning and connections in a world awash in data. Others note that studies in literature, history and politics provide graduates with a deep understanding of the world and, most important, of people—an invaluable asset in a business environment crowded with techies and number-crunchers. (Those working in sales are probably ahead of the curve: many have long recognized that salespeople with technical knowledge *and* arts backgrounds are best at explaining and pitching complex products and services to their non-technical customers.)

While philosophy and history majors can finally stop defending themselves at Thanksgiving dinner, it's the fine arts majors, the artists, who might have the most to teach us. Artists, we argue, hold the real keys to success in our modern world. Learning to do what they do can help us all succeed, achieve and solve problems.

But first, if we're going to convince you that you should act and think like an artist, we should probably all agree on what an artist is in the first place. When you hear the word *artist*, you probably think of someone like the young

Dr. Semple: a "painter." And we can see why. Painters' lives and work are familiar—they're not as foreign to us as other types of artists might be. It's tougher to understand an interpretive dancer swaying wildly on a Plexiglas cube, wearing nothing but a Lycra bodysuit and Kabuki face paint than it is to admire a pretty landscape. We recognize and appreciate some artists but not all artists.

Although judging art is subjective, talking about art and artists becomes meaningless unless we have some shared criteria. Despite that sensible notion, it can be hard to pin down a useful definition of "artist." A little Internet research quickly leads into murky debates about art and "genius." One of the most common theories shared by artists and art critics alike is that artists are individuals who create art. (Merriam-Webster's first definition is "a person who creates art.") And just to clarify, a number of pundits go on to point out that true art is work produced by real artists. It's hard to argue with that line of thinking. But it's about as helpful as the instructions for assembling Ikea furniture.

Sarah Thornton, a Canadian sociologist and arts journalist, interviewed visual artists for her book *33 Artists in 3 Acts*. Almost everyone she talked to, if they were willing to weigh in at all, had a different idea of what constitutes art and artists. In an earlier article, "What Is an Artist?" she gave her own opinion: "Perhaps it would help to consider what artists are not? Members of the general public often confuse artists with craftspeople. They assume that artists draw well and are gifted with their hands. Yet this definition is about 500 years out of date."

While medieval art patrons and enthusiasts (not to mention many earlier societies around the world) saw the distinction between art and craft, it was during the Italian Renaissance that the difference between them really began to take hold of the public imagination. More and more people began to appreciate that the works of Leonardo da Vinci and Michelangelo were different from those of the guys who painted grapes on wine decanters. Society embraced the notion that *true* art was work of inventiveness and originality *as well as* craftsmanship. Craftsmen (say, those who do the manual labour of building a sculpture, or the assistants who laboured in Rembrandt's workshop) produce things of high quality and value, but not originality. We may love the Shaker sewing tables that a fine woodworker produces, but because they are based on someone else's original design, they are craft rather than art, and their creators are artisans rather than artists.

Thornton goes on to observe that those we consider artists are also "professional thought-provokers" who produce works that communicate with others, works they hope will be seen and appreciated in a museum.

If we change "seen in a museum" to "find an audience," we're with Thornton. But like most people, Thornton is thinking only about painters and other visual artists. We'd like to broaden that definition a little. For the purposes of this discussion, here's how we are using the word *artist*:

Artists are people who authentically, creatively and originally express themselves. That's it.

Let's break it down.

1. *It's about expression.*

The expression may be an oil painting, a Ukrainian dance, a poem, a trumpet solo, a stained glass window, a comedy sketch or a million other possibilities. The medium isn't important. Artists have something of value to say and articulate it in a meaningful way. Artists communicate.

2. *It's about creativity and originality.*

We'll talk more about what creativity is in Chapter 1, but for now, it's important to point out that while all artists express themselves, all expression is not art. The guy who gives you the finger on the highway may be expressing himself, but that is not art. An installation of three thousand plastic middle fingers doused in fluorescent paint just might be. Artists create work that is original, thought-provoking and moving. They create something that is both new and lasting. That's what makes them artists.

3. *It's about authenticity.*

A true artist has to be authentic. Every song, every dance, every poem, every drawing is an artist saying, "This is what *I* am thinking." Their message may not be apparent, others may have to dig to find the meaning, but with true art, it's there. It's *the artist's* perspective, not *a* perspective.

In other words, if there isn't a little piece of their soul in their work, they're not artists.

Now that we've outlined what an artist is, you may be wondering *why* we should all be one. What is it about artists that gives them an edge in our modern world?

Let's start with expression. Artists are in the business of expressing themselves. But that's not so unusual today. *Lots* of people are expressing themselves. Technology has made it incredibly easy to share our views, our work and our lives with others. Whether it's a Facebook posting about a hamster, a tweet about the torture of a root canal, or an Instagram photo of a dinner plate, many people seem to be in the business of broadcasting their every waking minute.

This proliferation can make it a bit tricky if we are trying to get a message across, find an audience, sell a solution or just be heard. We're no longer competing for attention with the entertainment industry, marketers and artists of all kinds; we're trying to draw people's attention away from a million cat videos, a sea of blog posts and every new Scumbag Steve meme. We're operating in crowded, noisy world— what might be called the "expression economy."

And in the expression economy, it's easy to talk, but it's hard to get heard.

Let's face it, we all want and need to be heard. It doesn't matter if you're a six-year-old trying to get a bump in your allowance, a sixty-year-old who wants to connect with your neighbours, a new teacher trying to tame a prepubescent horde or a CEO who has to find additional revenue streams. If you want to convince anyone of anything or connect with others in a meaningful way, you have to communicate. And the fact that everyone out there is expressing himself or herself, even if it is just to say that lunch was pretty good today, means that it's more important than ever to express yourself effectively—in other words, in some way that sets you apart.

Thriving in the expression economy, we would argue, doesn't require a starring role on the Internet, but it does require learning from those who have made expression their life's work, from those who are truly brilliant at expression. It requires learning from the artistic process. And a large part of that is learning how artists nurture and expand their creativity.

Creativity is at the heart of every art form. It's almost ridiculously obvious to say that. It doesn't matter what type of art you participate in—trombone playing, sculpting, animation, or even (gulp) mime—if you're not creative, well, it's not really art. And it's boring.

We know, we know. Saying that the important thing we can learn from artists is creativity is like saying the most important thing swimmers can learn from fish is the ability to stay afloat. But why do we *need* to be more creative? Well, there's the fact that we are living in this world of non-stop expression. One of the ways to cut through the noise is to say something new, fresh and innovative, all of which demand a level of creativity. But it's more than that.

After years of thinking that the key to a successful life was following the rules and working hard, we are beginning to appreciate that the success of human endeavour is not so straightforward. Rapid-fire advancements in technology and the movement of labour and many secondary industries overseas are making us aware of the importance of innovation. As all the articles and books about the value of the liberal arts degrees suggest, we are also reawakening to the idea that we need, that in fact we are dependent upon, "soft skills." Connection, communication, imagination and originality are just as important as our ability to calculate and code.

In fact, that's why we—Chris and Scott—decided to name our company "The Art Of." While our original initial events focused on topics such as golfing and cooking, we have shifted our attention to the world of business: The Art of Marketing, The Art of Sales, The Art of Leadership, and The Art of Leadership for Women. Our events feature bestselling authors and world-renowned thought leaders. Their presentations are a lively blend of education and entertainment, of fascinating ideas and great storytelling. We consider them "artists" in their fields—creative minds who brilliantly express their original and authentic ideas and connect with their audiences in a powerful and helpful way.

Society's new-found appreciation for the "soft skills" has made people think differently about all aspects of life. As the world around us has shifted, we have begun to appreciate anew that creativity and creative thinking are at the heart of problem solving, scientific and medical advances, social and political improvement, and personal achievement and satisfaction. The more challenging our world becomes, the more important "thinking outside the box" becomes. As British educator and writer Ken Robinson says so powerfully in his book *Out of Our Minds*, this intensified appreciation of creativity has reshaped our landscape: "The whole world is engulfed in a revolution." And in this brave new world, we *all* need to think more creatively.

- Moms need to be more creative.
- Dads need to be more creative.
- Shopkeepers need to be more creative.
- Teachers need to be more creative.
- Payroll clerks need to be more creative.
- Students need to be more creative.
- Everyone needs to be more creative.

In today's workplace it is especially important that creativity flourish. It should no longer be considered the exclusive domain of the advertising department or of interior design companies. It shouldn't be happening only in our cultural industries and architecture firms. If we want our companies and workplaces to be efficient, productive and competitive (not to mention exciting, fulfilling places to work), creativity needs to be encouraged in jobs and roles that have not traditionally been defined as creative.

CEOs need to be more creative, as do fundraisers, receptionists, lawyers, finance people, HR departments, IT specialists, and on and on. And they all *can* be. (Okay, we admit it. Accountants who get a little *too* creative can sometimes end up in jail. There are limits.)

It's not as if this is really news. Leonardo da Vinci, a man who turned his remarkable mind to science and math as well as painting, would no doubt be shocked that we've assigned the idea of creativity to artists alone. And even in the last hundred years, our most brilliant, world-changing thinkers have tried to draw our attention to the power of creativity. Einstein, for one, talked about its importance in his work. "When I examine myself and my methods of thought," he once explained to a friend, "I come close to the conclusion that the gift of imagination has meant more to me than any talent for absorbing absolute knowledge." Creative thought appears to be key, whether it's in formulating the theory of relativity or pulling off a stress-free family car trip.

So that covers expression and creativity. What about that third point: authenticity? Artistic authenticity also has some important lessons for us. It's usually not a great idea—for your relationships with others, or for the good of your soul—to run around saying things you don't believe in or living a life that is somehow a charade. As the saying goes, "Be yourself. Everyone else is taken." Moreover, being authentic affects your ability to be creative, an idea that we explore in more depth in Chapter 7.

You may now be thinking, *I get it, I get it. Be more creative. But how?*

First, you have to recognize your own inner artist. While many of us may feel that closest we get to an artistic endeavour is when we choose shoes to go with our pants, we all have some innate creative ability. The notion that everyone *should* be an artist doesn't mean that we have to turn a slab of marble into the *Venus de Milo*. (Where would we put all those statues anyhow?) But we can nurture what spark we have by doing what artists do. In the following pages, we'll look at artists' habits, attitudes and behaviours. We'll see how these foster their creativity, reinforce their authenticity, facilitate communication and keep them producing art. And we'll discuss how these same tools can help the rest of us achieve our goals, develop something new, or be successful in our professional and personal lives. In other words, how we can think like artists.

Everyone is an artist. Or at least we *can* be.

The artist never entirely knows. We guess. We may be wrong, but we take leap after leap in the dark."

—Agnes de Mille, choreographer

CONGRATULATIONS, YOU'RE AN ARTIST

I n the Introduction we talked about society's renewed appreciation for the importance of creativity in all aspects of work and life. We argued that we can learn much from those who have dedicated their lives to creative pursuits—the artists. And we said that we all have the ability to be artists.

That might be a hard sell for those of you who have still not gotten over the trauma of your first botched Paint by Number kit. You may feel that you're as creative as a box of saltines. But that's where you are wrong. Everyone has creative ability; everyone is, in a sense, an artist. As Steven Pinker, Harvard psychology professor and author of *How the Mind Works*, puts it: "All of us are creative. Every time we stick a handy object under the leg of a wobbly table or think up a new way to bribe a child into his pajamas, we have used our faculties to create a novel outcome." Pinker may be overstating a bit. The first person who stuck something under the chair was being creative; the rest of us are just followers after all. But we understand what Pinker is getting at. It's strange to think of bribing a child as an act of creativity, but when it dawns on you that the promise of "helping" dad shave in the morning might just get your child to bed in time for you to watch the rest of the game, it may not seem like art, but it is an original idea of enormous value.

Part of what makes people think that they can't possibly be creative types is that they are often blind to the creative thinking around them. They recognize the artistic genius of an Andy Warhol or an Amy Winehouse, and appreciate the innovative brilliance of a Thomas Edison or a Steve Jobs. But much far-less glamorous work, like everyday problem solving, is evidence of creativity too.

Not long ago, we were talking with some neighbours about how exhausting it was to wait up for teenage kids to make sure they got home at the agreed-upon time. One neighbour said that he didn't have a problem with that. He was using his parents' trick to get the sleep he needed. He grew up in the country and his parents had been farmers most of their lives. Even if they wanted to, they weren't able to sleep in. So they headed to bed early. When their son got to be a teen, however, they wanted to make sure he adhered to a curfew that was a good deal later than their preferred bedtime. So they set their bedroom alarm clock to five minutes past the curfew time and went to sleep. The teen had to get home in time to turn the alarm clock off. If he was late, and his parents were awoken by the alarm, he was grounded for a week. Simple. Effective. Ingenious. Creative.

Dr. John Semple, in his *Globe and Mail* profile and in his conversation with us, agrees that creative thinking is all around us. "The idea that creativity is part of everyday thinking is something I use all the time," he says, "specifically in my capacity for dealing with abstract ideas. I find a lot of people fear facing abstract notions, and will retreat to known components." (He notes that this is why scientific research often advances only incrementally.) But a painter is trained to face a blank canvas, and deal with it head-on. While he hastens to point out that there can't really be any self-expression in surgery—"you have to stick to the plan"—he notes than in medical research, being comfortable with or attracted to abstract ideas can lead to looking at things in original ways: "That might be in terms of microvascular blood flow, or different ways the body can heal or be encouraged to heal."

There's no doubt that many of us are not the "artists" we once were. For starters, most of us don't use our imaginations the way we used to. Children are imaginative geniuses. Just spend a little time with a four-year-old, and you'll enter the world of chocolate ponds and pet dragons and cabbages that can fly. Self-driving cars? Four-year-olds have understood the possibilities ever since the Model T hit the road. Living on the moon? Of course. Communication with dolphins or apes or bees? Four-year-olds are surprised that *you* are surprised that these things are now known realities. As pediatric psychologist Mark Bowers observes, "Creativity is at a high point from age three to five."

And the amazing thing about the rich fantasy world of children is that no one shows them how to enter. They are *born* into it. Indeed, educators and developmental psychologists have provided plenty of evidence that the imagination plays a key role in the way children learn about the world. Imaginative play is how children recognize that their thoughts differ from those of others, and it encourages empathy, impulse control, social skills and the expression of emotion. Playing "let's pretend" has also been shown to help vocabulary, improve academic readiness and enhance intellectual curiosity. And not surprisingly, children who engage in more imaginative play demonstrate stronger creative abilities when they become adults. So all of those imaginary friends, all of those talking gerbils, all of those living room carpets that are really quicksand are an important part of our cognitive development—and of our future creative lives.

Even as children learn about the world and replace their role-playing and imaginative space with knowledge, facts and practical skills, they tend to engage in far more creative activities than most adults allow themselves. Who among us hasn't displayed nascent thespian talents in a grade-school production of *The Three Little Pigs*?

And who hasn't belted out "Frosty the Snowman" at the annual holiday showcase? As kids, we painted and drew and sculpted (although our parents were usually pretty stingy with the Carrara marble). We may have spent days or weeks designing our Halloween costumes or hours pouring our hearts into poetry or song lyrics. We may have built elaborate Lego empires or ingenious blanket forts. We might have taken dance lessons or taught ourselves how to play "Takin' Care of Business" on the guitar.

Unfortunately, for many of us, those artistic pursuits fell by the wayside as we grew older. Report cards and competition perhaps made us aware that we weren't as good at some of those things as other kids were, so we backed off. We may have been told that such activities were "only for fun," that we needed to concentrate on more serious matters. Or we may have simply been defeated by the repeated question, "What do you want to be when you grow up?" Chances are if we said we wanted to be a painter or a musician or an actor, we heard that those were "unrealistic" goals at best. Actuarial accounting, internal medicine, personal injury law—now those are real careers!

International education advisor Ken Robinson has argued in his books and TED talks that our education system, created to address the needs of a past society and not those of our current world, actually beats the creativity out of us. The acquisition of knowledge, the command of facts, the mastery of rational thought and the following of rules have become all-important—and have made creativity an unwelcome guest in the classroom. (Music and visual arts are usually regarded as the entertaining "extras" in a student's school day.)

Robinson notes that a number of studies have shown that teachers put creative students at the bottom of their "favourites" list (more about this in Chapter 8), which reminds us of a story we recently heard from a friend who was trying to get her four-year-old son into a prestigious private school. This was going to be an uphill battle—especially after the little guy told her what happened during an entrance assessment with a school administrator. The interview involved completing a number of "tests." In one, the boy was asked to reproduce the shapes that had been drawn on a piece of paper. "Did you have trouble drawing the shapes?" asked his mother. "Nah, I didn't draw them," he said. "Why not?" said his mother, alarmed. "That would have been dumb," he said. "They had all those shapes already. I drew them some *new* ones."

Who could argue with that logic? Faced with a boring triangle, the little guy had let loose with wild trapezoids and ballooning parabolas. Very creative. Very not-what-the-school-was-looking-for. He didn't get in.

So, for most of us, a good deal of our imaginative, artistic life has been forgotten in our childhood closets, along with Lego and outgrown clothes. And yet even people who have left artistic ambitions behind have not lost their creative selves or abandoned their creative impulses entirely. If they had, how to explain the incredible success of companies like League of Rock? Terry Moshenberg's brilliant idea was to create a way for lawyers, marketers, teachers and stay-at-home parents (and anyone else) to embrace their inner Bruce Springsteens. Sign up, pay your dough and you get to be in a band for ten weeks.

Each band is mentored by an experienced producer, and at the end of the ten weeks, they perform live in front of family and friends. League of Rock delivers the complete rock experience (excluding heroin, groupies and "back-stage passes").

Many Rolling Stones wannabes have flocked to League of Rock because it lets them rediscover the creative and expressive spirit they had in their youth. It allows them to literally be the rock stars they dreamed of being before mortgage payments and the BabyBjörn got in the way. The marketing campaign cleverly underlined the attraction of this creative outlet for the responsible business types. "Stick it to the man!" the posters declared. "Even if you *are* the man."

Of course, League of Rock isn't the only avenue for cubicle dwellers and the like to return to the artistic pursuits of their youth. Technology is now making it much easier to re-engage. Cellphone cameras and Photoshop have made it possible for everyone to be Ansel Adams when the mood strikes. YouTube offers thousands of DIY music and art tutorials. Online writing workshops and writers' circles are popping up all over the Web. Word processors everywhere are filling up with first-draft novels. And then there's the frighteningly enduring appeal of karaoke.

What Moshenberg and others have recognized is that for most adults the artistic spirit never left; only the ability to realize it did.

Of course, being creative is not just about picking up a paintbrush or a guitar. As we discussed in the Introduction, creativity can happen and should happen in the home and in the workplace. It is the key to problem solving and innovation. You may never sign up for League of Rock, but you need to exercise your creative side nonetheless.

The good news about creative ability is that we all have some, even if we've neglected it, and we can all improve it. But before looking at how to improve, we'll examine more closely at how creativity works.

Numerous psychologists and researchers have rejected the idea that creative geniuses are struck out of the blue by a visit from the muse. Samuel Coleridge and Edgar Allan Poe may have implied—or flat-out claimed—that their writing was the product of flashes of inspiration, fully realized ideas and lines of poetry popping unbidden into their minds, but careful reading of their journals and other evidence suggests that their work was the end result of a long process of trial and error, of writing and rewriting, of good old-fashioned slogging.

And yet, obviously there is something about the work of great artists that is exceptional. How do we explain that sort of creative thinking, those fabulous ideas?

In the mid-1920s, social psychologist Graham Wallas put forth one of the first theories about how the creative process works. It has stood the test of time surprisingly well. He suggested that there were five phases. First, planning or *preparation*, where the problem to be solved was set out. The next was *incubation*, a period of rest from thinking about the problem consciously. That was followed by *intimation*, the sensation that an idea is about to pop into your head, and *illumination*, the period during which the idea presents itself, and we become conscious of it. (Intimation and illumination are often considered two parts of the same stage.) Finally, there is *verification*, in which ideas are selected, tested and revised.

A great deal of research and study has centred on incubation and illumination, but the preparation and verification stages—not so much. These phases are hard to study because they tend to happen over longer periods of time (and test subjects are loath to spend days lying in brain-imaging machines). They also seem a good deal less mysterious: planning and reworking are things most of us do all of the time. But it's important to note that the preparation stage usually refers to a problem or challenge that's been identified—in other words, creativity doesn't usually come out of nowhere. In fact, the notion that constraints inhibit creativity appears to be misguided. Often hurdles or limitations get the creative juices flowing. If that sounds counterintuitive, just think of Michelangelo being asked to do a painting on the ceiling of the Sistine Chapel. The relatively small space is dark, and the ceiling is curved in a way that means that viewers are going to be looking at the artwork at decidedly unusual angles—never mind the fact that he was going to have to lie on his back, metres above the floor, for years. Michelangelo addressed these problems not just adequately but brilliantly.

And that final phase of creative thinking, verification, while not sounding as sexy an idea as generation, is absolutely essential to producing ideas that have value. Once we've generated lots of ideas, we winnow through them and pick the ones that look the most promising—what some theorists call "selection." Then we test them, polish them, revise them. In other words, we engage in some exploration and tinkering.

Creative geniuses, it's worth noting, are really, really good at this last stage of the creative process. They have sophisticated levels of discernment and are skilled at recognizing which ideas have value and which don't. (If we look to creativity in practice—innovation—we can come up with all sorts of examples of when that last phase is botched. Product ideas that were original or "new" but didn't have much value or meaning and have sunk into oblivion. Carbonated yoghurt. Cheeseburgers in a can. Cheetos-flavoured lip balm. All real products, we kid you not. All mercifully no longer available for purchase. And all proving that *selection is important*.)

Ken Robinson notes that creativity can only flourish when we give ourselves time to move through the necessary phases. If we focus on selection too early, our internal critic can inhibit our ideas guy.

And what about the creation of those ideas? The incubation period is key to the mystery of creativity. It's a time when the conscious brain is absorbed with other tasks—say, planting your garden or shampooing your hair. In other words, it's time when you aren't looking at a problem head-on or thinking about it in a deliberate way. Some psychologists believe this period of unconscious associative processing allows the unconscious to take over and make connections that your conscious brain might reject as illogical or irrelevant. Others believe that a period of not thinking about the problem at hand allows you to forget about misleading information so that your unconscious brain can play with only the most meaningful parts of the puzzle.

Other psychologists and researchers focus on convergent–divergent thinking when talking about the process of idea generation, noting that divergent thinking, the ability to generate many possible answers to a question, is the initial stage of creativity, and is followed by convergent thinking, focusing on a single answer, winnowing down the options. The theory of conceptual blending posits that creativity arises from the intersection of different frames of reference, like the process by which we come up with metaphors and analogies.

These and other ways of describing the creative process are complemented by the research of neurologists who have been trying to use brain imaging and other methods of studying brain function to determine what's going on in that incubation period, how we access that state and how it connects to idea generation.

And while this whole process is still essentially a mystery, we are uncovering a few interesting facts about how our grey matter functions. Studies of the brain using functional MRI machines have shown that when creative thinking and doing happen, activity in part of the prefrontal cortex quiets. This area—the dorsolateral prefrontal cortex (DLPFC)—is a part of the executive control network of the brain and is thought to be involved with self-censoring, impulse control and inhibition, among other things. It appears that when this calm master of control is sent on lunch break, the imagination has a bit more room to play. This area more or less shuts down completely when we enter the REM cycle of sleep—the phase during which we dream. So perhaps not surprisingly, studies have shown that people demonstrate more creative ability immediately after a period of REM sleep. The DLPFC is also an area of the brain that develops quite late, so it really should be no surprise that most people are considerably more imaginative at six than at sixty. (Apparently we can't entirely blame teachers and parents for the loss of our fantasy worlds.)

Rex Jung, a neuropsychologist and professor at the University of New Mexico, is one of the researchers who have been studying brain images to see what happens during creative thought. Some of his research has focused on what parts of the brain seem to be most engaged when subjects are involved in the incubation and illumination phases. His brain-imaging studies suggest that when we are in the incubation phase, parts of the default-mode network become active. These are the areas of the brain that take over when you are at rest or not focused on a task, and they are especially active when you are daydreaming or allowing your mind to wander. Interviewed for the *Atlantic*, Jung puts it this way: "You're looking inward instead of solving the problems of the world." And when this part of the brain is engaged, he suggests, ideas are allowed to connect and cross-pollinate in ways they might not have otherwise. But when you are ready to express that idea (Wallas's illumination phase), Jung has observed, the cognitive or "executive" control network, areas of the brain that appear to be involved with planning, directing and implementing thought, kick into gear.

Jung noted that interactions between these areas seem to be the key to creativity: "We see that the most highly creative people flip easily between the two and are better able to modulate these networks." A number of other studies have also shown that these two networks seem to work closely together during intense periods of creativity. Jung's studies have also suggested that highly creative people not only come up with more ideas, they come up with more good ones too.

Right about now, you may be feeling that all of this is well and good, but knowing about how your brain works is not going to help you have "eureka!" moments any more than understanding how your fridge works is going to make it any colder. But you may be wrong. It seems that we may be able to tinker with our mental machinery. A 2008 experiment conducted by Johns Hopkins researchers put jazz musicians into fMRI machines and asked them to start improvising. What the researchers noticed was that just as the musicians started playing, the DLPFC area went quiet—as if the jazz artists had simply turned it off. While the musicians were no doubt unaware that they were doing this (and they certainly weren't conscious of what parts of their brains were lighting up on the imaging screens), this fascinating phenomenon suggests the rest of us might also be able to move ourselves into a creative headspace at will.

The key may be learning to let our minds wander. In a *New Yorker* article entitled "How Caffeine Can Cramp Creativity," psychologist Maria Konnikova writes:

> *Creative insights and imaginative solutions often occur when we stop working on a particular problem and let our mind move on to something unrelated. In one recent study, participants showed marked improvements on a task requiring creative thought—thinking of alternative uses for a common object, such as a newspaper—after they had engaged in a different, undemanding task that facilitated mind wandering. The more their mind wandered when they stepped away, the better they fared at being creative. In fact, the benefit was not*

seen at all when the subjects engaged in an unrelated but demanding task.

Konnikova goes on to explain that research has shown that caffeine interferes with creativity by focusing our thoughts and preventing our mind from wandering.

What we can take away from all of this is that there is a strong scientific argument for staring out the office window and wondering where to take your next holiday instead of obsessing about that new building design you are supposed to be working on. Part of thinking more creatively is letting yourself go a little.

And there's even more scientific evidence that we are able to improve our creative muscle. Researchers at the University of Reading in the U.K. and the University of Minnesota discovered that when people do warm-up exercises in creative thinking, they perform much better in subsequent creative-thinking tasks. In the study, subjects were asked to generate alternative uses for a common object, like a ping-pong ball or a brick. They did this for as little as ten minutes. After the warm-up, they were asked to solve insight puzzles along with other tests of creative thinking. Those who had done the alternative-uses exercises did much better at these tasks than those who had done word-association warm-ups or no warm-ups at all.

The usefulness of creative-thinking exercises in improving our mental flexibility was also studied using fMRI machines by researchers at the Ministry of Education and the School of

Psychology in Chongqing, China. Images were made of brain activity when the subjects were at rest. The participants then engaged in an alternative-uses exercise and were put back into the fMRI. The images of their brains at rest *after* they had been generating novel ideas for using household items or for making a child's toy more fun showed much stronger communication between two areas of the brain—one that appears to be involved when the imagination is employed in story generation or improvisation, and one that is active in linking or expanding ideas and in metaphorical thinking. This increased connectivity then appeared to produce much better results in subsequent creativity tests—particularly for those who had scored lowest on baseline creativity at the start of the study.

What is really going on in the twists and folds of our brain tissue when we are being creative is still essentially a mystery. But these scientific studies do support the anecdotal evidence that we can actually improve our creativity power. It seems that, with some effort, we can put ourselves into mental states that allow for divergent thought. And we can strengthen our creative muscle by using it more often.

In the following chapters, we are going to look at some of the ways artists and innovators access their imagination and generate ideas. (It's also worth noting that there are a host of seminars, self-help books and online articles that provide tips and techniques for gaining access to the unconscious wellspring of creativity.) But it's important to recognize that each of us has our own way of getting the little mental break that allows our creative self to blossom. Some are downright strange. Painter Francis Bacon, a heavy drinker, didn't credit inebriation with releasing his creative energy, but rather the post-binge period: "I often like working with a hangover," he said, "because my mind is crackling with energy and I think very clearly." If you substitute the words *energy* with *pain* and *working* with *lying on the couch moaning like a plague victim*, then many of us have a lot in common with Francis. But we're not getting much creative thinking done.

Bacon is not the only artist who had a liking for mind-altering substances, but most have less dramatic ways of finding inspiration and doing what they do. Adopting some of their habits, attitudes and outlooks can help us become our best creative selves and rediscover the natural artists we were when we were young. But first we may need to change how we see ourselves in order to let that happen.

In other words, we may need to reinvent ourselves.

Don't be afraid to scrap all your hard work and planning and do it differently at the last minute. It's easier to hold on to an idea because you're afraid to admit you were wrong than to let it go."

—Polly Morgan, artist

REINVENT YOURSELF

D ecades ago neurologists discovered that the two hemispheres of our brains appeared to be associated with different skills and abilities. The left half seemed to be the home of language, logic, reasoning, and analytical thinking; the right half, of intuition and creativity. Most psychologists and neurologists now consider that left brain/right brain distinction to be too simplistic—the brain continues to surprise researchers, and just about everyone else who uses one, with its flexibility and interconnectedness. But the idea that some people have more dominant natural inclinations to "left-brain" skills or "right-brain" attributes has been a useful way to understand how individuals operate in life and work. For example, those who are strong in left-brain skills fare well in business and in running systems and organizations. These types have been in charge of many companies—and in charge of much of our world—and frankly, they still are. But that's beginning to change.

Daniel Pink, in his bestseller *A Whole New Mind: Why Right-Brainers Will Rule the Future*, explains:

> *The last few decades have belonged to a certain type of person with a certain kind of mind— computer programmers who could crank code, lawyers who could craft contracts, MBAs who could crunch numbers. But the keys to the Kingdom are changing hands. The future belongs to a very different kind of person with a very different kind of mind—creators and empathizers, pattern recognizers, and meaning makers. These people—artists, inventors, designers, storytellers, caregivers, consolers, big picture thinkers—will now reap society's richest rewards and share its greatest joys.*

Sad, isn't it? You were told to study hard and go into something with a future, like computer programming or accounting, only to find that, according to Pink and an increasing number of thinkers, this sort of work can be automated or outsourced to other countries with lower wages. With today's abundance of products and services, it's not the people who can crunch the numbers who are getting ahead, but the people who can creatively interpret them.

The happy news, however, is that no matter what your field of study or your occupation, you can join those creative thinkers, those right-brainers: the inventors and designers, the storytellers and the artists. You are a creative being; you just have to start considering yourself one to start being one. Easier said than done, we know. But the first step is moving past the stereotypes surrounding creative people.

A number of years ago, Apple launched a critically successful TV commercial dubbed "The Crazy Ones." You've surely seen it. It features a compelling black-and-white visual of eighteen brilliant personalities: Albert Einstein, Bob Dylan, Martin Luther King, Jr., Richard Branson, John Lennon and Yoko Ono, Buckminster Fuller, Thomas Edison, Muhammad Ali, Ted Turner, Maria Callas, Mahatma Gandhi, Amelia Earhart, Alfred Hitchcock, Martha Graham, Jim Henson, Frank Lloyd Wright, and Pablo Picasso.

It acknowledges their creative contributions and describes the group as misfits, rebels, troublemakers—as crazy. The commercial goes on to celebrate their genius and their impact in changing the world.

The spot has been applauded for years and saw a resurgence in popularity with the passing of Steve Jobs. From an advertising perspective, it's one of our all-time favourites, and it certainly helped put Apple back on the

map. No doubt about it, in marketing terms, it was a bona
fide success

In other ways, however, it was an absolute failure. It
failed because it reinforced how those in roles traditionally defined as "uncreative" see creativity: as the exclusive
domain of those who are crazy and rebellious. In other
words, if you're a misfit, you're creative, and if you're not,
well, don't bother trying because you are going to embarrass yourself. Mahatma Gandhi was a creative thinker.
You're just Hank, the managing director of a small not-for-
profit. Get a grip.

The spot has been applauded for years and saw a resurgence in popularity with the unfortunate passing of Steve
Jobs. From an advertising perspective, it's one of our
all-time favourites, and it certainly helped put Apple back
on the map. No doubt about it, in marketing terms, it was
bona fide success.

In other ways, however, it was an absolute failure.

It failed because it reinforced how those in roles traditionally defined as "uncreative" see creativity: as the
exclusive domain of those who are crazy and rebellious.
In other words, if you're a misfit, you're creative, and if
you're not, well, don't bother trying because you are going
to embarrass yourself. Mahatma Gandhi was a creative
thinker. You're just Hank, a managing director for a small
not-for-profit. Get a grip.

But Apple could have just as easily done a spot called
"The Quiet Ones." It might have featured the English

novelist Anthony Trollope and American poets T. S. Eliot and Wallace Stevens, who worked for most of their adult lives for the post office, a bank and an insurance company, respectively. (Wallace Stevens loved his job at the insurance company. He credited the regularity and structure of the work with allowing him to release his creative side when he wasn't in the office.) Or French post-Impressionist painter Henri Rousseau, whose most famous works feature dreamlike jungle scenes, despite the fact that he never left France and laboured for decades as a customs officer. Or singer-songwriter and lead guitarist Randy Bachman, who was a founding member of The Guess Who and Bachman-Turner Overdrive, but, as a Mormon, focused on the rock and roll part of sex, drugs and rock and roll. (Talking on his CBC Radio show *Vinyl Tap*, he once laughed about a letter from a fan who wanted him to write a book about his wild and crazy life on the road. "Yeah, wrong guy," he said.)

Being creative isn't about being a wild one. As we discussed in the previous chapter, everyone has the ability to be creative, and to increase their creativity. Everyone can think and act more like an artist. Part of the challenge is to allow yourself to grow and change, to adopt a new or even slightly altered version of yourself.

Some years ago, we were at a conference. A dinner had been arranged off-site, and a number of us were talking about the best way to get there. Someone mentioned that since there was a subway stop right at the conference hotel, and the restaurant was steps away from another stop, it might be fastest to take public transportation. One of our group began shaking her head even before the speaker finished. "No," she said immediately, "I don't take the subway anymore. That's not me."

That's not me. It seemed like such a strange response, and we weren't entirely sure what she meant by it. Perhaps she intended it as an expression of her success, to say that she had arrived at a point in her life where she travelled only by luxury automobile or by taxi. Or maybe she had had a bad experience on the subway and wasn't comfortable on it. Either way, we couldn't help feel that this was sad. There is nothing wrong with having a preferred mode of transportation, but defining yourself as a person "who doesn't take the subway" seemed to suggest limits rather than power, a reduced life rather than one of self-fulfillment or luxury. This woman, it seemed to us, was creating boxes for herself, eliminating choice and possibility, even in this very small way. If she defined herself by ways she would not travel, how many other narrow categories had she placed on herself? We wouldn't be the least surprised if she thought of herself as "not creative" as well.

But coming up with restrictive ideas about ourselves is, unfortunately, a natural impulse. And it starts early. Often in school we get handed a label. Perhaps it is "nerd" or "jock." Maybe it's "learning disabled" or "hyperactive." Sometimes it's seemingly positive: "the nice kid," "the good student," "the responsible one." It takes a being with superhuman inner strength not to internalize these kinds of definitions. But as we enter our early adulthood, we may recognize that we shouldn't be defined solely by others. We may feel the need to "find ourselves." Sometimes this search requires trips to Nepal, living out of a backpack and infrequent bathing. Sometimes embarking on courses of study or trying our hand at different jobs does the trick. Sometimes we come to understand a bit more about ourselves through our romantic relationships and friendships. But once we've decided who we are and what we want to do (even if that is as straightforward as "make a comfortable income and get a schnauzer"), we set off to make this happen.

It's a natural impulse, but it can lead to a calcification of how we see ourselves—and how we identify our talents, our strengths and our capabilities. "I'm a couch potato." "I'm an accountant." "I'm an outdoors person." "I'm a mom." We tend to label ourselves according to our profession or the most dominant activity in our lives. And if these things are not generally considered creative, unconsciously or unconsciously we may think of ourselves as "not creative."

But if we want to have real power in our lives and real creative potential, we have to think of ourselves in new ways, allow ourselves new experiences. We need to give ourselves permission to start again, to reinvent ourselves, even in small ways. What's more, we need to commit to the process of reinvention; in other words, to reinvent the way we think about things more or less continually. (We know, that sounds exhausting, but it usually isn't. It's energizing.

And a better way to fight boredom and ennui than buying new shoes or watching endless rounds of do-it-yourself TV shows.)

Artists provide great examples of reinvention. Becoming an artist, engaging one's creative self, is, after all, a choice. Art journalist Sarah Thornton notes in her essay "What Is an Artist?" that several curators she knows are of the opinion that gifted artists are people who have no other alternative than to make art. But, she continues, "I've interviewed more than 100 artists for a book I'm researching . . . and none have given me the impression that their occupation was an unavoidable fate." In other words, they are not compelled by biology or unseen forces; they choose to do what they do.

But we all make choices about our professions. More important is the way in which artists work. We talk about artists, musicians, actors and so on "growing" throughout their careers. Some change the medium they work in. Jeff Koons, best known for his enormous sculptures of balloon animals, studied painting as an art student. Picasso, known primarily for his paintings and etchings, also sculpted and did pottery, and wrote over three hundred poems and two plays.

It's not hard to think of songwriters, musicians and singers who have done this as well. Aretha Franklin and a host of others moved from gospel to Motown. Kelly Clarkson and Taylor Swift started as country stars. John Cougar Mellencamp and Alanis Morissette had embarrassing beginnings as teen pop idols. Elvis Costello is famous for baffling his fans by moving from genre to genre as his interests shift. And Bob Dylan shocked the folk music world when he went electric.

And then there are all of the artists who work in multiple media—Lady Gaga and Ice Cube, who are singers and songwriters but also actors. Robert De Niro, who acts and paints. Sam Shepard—award-winning playwright and actor. And perhaps the most impressive chameleon of all—Steve Martin. Martin started his career as a comedic writer on *The Smothers Brothers Comedy Hour*. He parlayed that into a hugely successful career as a stand-up comedian. From there, he became an actor. While acting, he wrote a play, adapted screenplays and began to direct and produce. He wrote essays for the *New Yorker*. Then he published a novella, two novels, a children's book and a memoir. And just to make sure he really can't be pigeon-holed, Steve Martin also plays the banjo, has performed and recorded with the likes of Earl Scruggs, Dolly Parton, Edie Brickell, and the Steep Canyon Rangers, *and* has curated an exhibit of the paintings of Lawren Harris for the Hammer Museum in Los Angeles.

But for most artists, reinvention is more subtle. While some talented folks move from acting to painting, or from oil painting to sculpture, most artists work in one medium or a few closely connected ones (drawing, painting and printmaking, for example). For artists, the most important kind of reinvention is about the evolution of ideas, about breaking new ground in technique and approach.

Sometimes this results in a switch in the style in which they work. Many of our most influential avant-garde visual artists started out painting and sculpting in a realistic style before exploring new approaches. (The early works of Picasso, Emily Carr and Andy Warhol might surprise you.) Most visual artists—as well as novelists, poets and musicians—move through different styles and phases as the years unfold. Being open to new ideas and new ways to look at the world is an important part of creating works of originality and value. Artists don't simply do the same thing over and over and over.

Perhaps some of the best examples of artists reinventing themselves are the lives of actors. With each new character they portray, actors step into fresh imaginative worlds. The best have an amazing ability to change it up—to seemingly inhabit a new skin, with distinct mannerisms, movements and speech. Think Meryl Streep as a Holocaust survivor, as Julia Child, as a hippie mom and as a thinly fictionalized Anna Wintour. Or Daniel Day-Lewis—a quadriplegic musician but also Abraham Lincoln. As Benedict Cumberbatch has observed about the transformations that an actor puts himself through, "The further you get away from yourself, the more challenging it is. Not to be in your comfort zone is great fun."

Ron Tite knows first-hand about the process of reinvention when you are a performer. Ron has been a stand-up comedian for over fifteen years (although today his focus is his content marketing agency and his work as a speaker). Part of the "charm," he says, of doing stand-up is that, along the way, you are bound to encounter inebriated audience members who want to provide real-time feedback on the material you've spent days or weeks preparing. They shout from the back, talk loudly to the people around them, and generally try to steal the spotlight by providing additional zingers. Usually hecklers just need to be ignored, but sometimes their interruptions offer the opportunity for the comedian to get a few extra laughs. Good comedians allow their acts to get sidetracked from time to time if the opportunity for humour is there, which means every performance is likely to be a little different.

So what's the point here? The point is that for an actor or live performer, each and every performance is new. It's a *reinvention*. And it is precisely this ability to tackle each performance as something new that brings that performance to life. (You realize this any time you watch an actor or musician who seems to be "phoning it in," perhaps composing a grocery list as they go through their lines. Those are the kinds performances that have you wanting to jab a ballpoint pen into your own eyeball, just for the distraction. And they sure aren't art!)

Likewise, for the sculptor, the painter, the fashion designer, the dancer, each work is a new invention, with fresh ideas. As with other types of artistic endeavours, as soon as a novel, a play or a poem becomes formulaic, derivative or repetitive, it ceases to be considered art. As author and editor Robert McCrum has said, "As a writer, you are always starting out afresh. Age and experience may teach you some tricks, but it will not touch your work with magic."

Artists also provide some encouraging examples of why "it's never too late."

In today's literary world, there's a certain cachet to the "wunderkind" writer—that twenty-something recent grad who has just produced a novel that is making the reading world stand up and take notice, and at the same time making vast swathes of the population feel inadequate. (Eleanor Catton's *The Luminaries* springs to mind. Catton's second novel, it won the prestigious Man Booker Prize when the author was a mere twenty-eight years old.) The music world is even more in love with the cult of youth—think sixteen-year-old Lorde setting iTunes on fire. (Try not to think about the teenage Britney Spears.) And, of course, no one loves youth more than Hollywood.

Starting young is the norm for most writers, actors, painters, musicians and so on. But that doesn't mean you've missed the boat if you haven't paid much attention to your creative self since you played the part of a carrot in your grade three "healthy eating" skit. You don't have to be young to start a creative life or just to start thinking creatively. Scotland's most successful contemporary painter, Jack Vettriano, worked in educational research, among other things, before he took up painting seriously at the age of thirty-six. Dostoyevsky wrote *Crime and*

Punishment at forty-five and *The Brothers Karamazov* at fifty-nine. And British author Mary Wesley started writing in her late fifties and had her first adult novel published at seventy-one.

So you can be an artist, or start thinking like one, even if you are well on your way to reading glasses and comfortable shoes. (Still feel you are not flexible enough to change? Just remember that in 2015, at the age of fifty-six, Barbie turned herself from a freakishly leggy and lean figurine into the much more realistic "Curvy Barbie." And *she's* made of rigid plastic.)

What we're saying is that reinventing yourself is really a two-part process. It's allowing yourself to think or act differently and then actually acting like an artist—employing the kind of constant reinvention that artists engage in.

Does reinventing yourself as a creative person mean you need to wear a week's worth of stubble and a knitted cap? Anyone who has worked in the marketing or advertising business knows how often people seem to confuse looking like a "creative" with actually being creative. These sorts show up late, dress like thrift-shop mavens and generally display an impressive level of self-confidence, as if they were, at any moment, about to find a way to achieve world peace. Or, at the very least, sell a remarkable amount of mayonnaise. Are there creative geniuses out there who look and behave a little differently from the mainstream? Of course there are. But their behaviours and appearances are a side effect of their brilliance, not the other way around. You don't become an artist or increase your creativity by refusing to wear shoes or feigning a love for film noir.

No, as Benedict Cumberbatch is likely to tell you, acting like a creative person means stepping outside your comfort zone. That doesn't necessarily mean you have to take up flamenco or pottery. But it does mean doing things that you might not ordinarily do, even if it's just taking the subway, reading a different sort of book or spending time in another country.

In fact, travel has actually been linked to increased creativity. It turns out that changing up your environment is one of the best ways to start the creative juices flowing. Columbia Business School professor Adam Galinsky has spent much of his career studying the effects of travel on creative work (covered in a thoughtful article by journalist Brent Crane in the *Atlantic*). His investigations suggest that the simple act of *immersing* yourself in a foreign environment, exposing yourself to new and different places, people, customs and ways of life, exercises the brain's cognitive flexibility, its "ability to jump between different ideas, a key component of creative thinking." Galinsky's studies have followed this correlation in fashion designers, as well as business executives.

Galinsky's work is supported by Wenfu Li, a professor of psychology at Southwest University, who has also found that those who possess "openness to experience" (by which he means new experiences) score higher on the

Williams Scale (developed in 1993 to gauge creativity in individuals) than those who don't. While Li's work also shows that there is an innate component to creativity, he is quick to point out that "openness to experience" is something everyone can work at improving.

Our good friend Mitch Joel is someone clearly open to new experiences and embracing reinvention. Mitch started his working life as a music journalist and publisher of two music magazines. He also co-launched Distort Entertainment, the only hardcore punk and metal music label in Canada to have major label distribution. But he didn't stop there. He used what he learned in this early phase of his working life reinvent his career. He is now one of the top digital visionaries in the country, if not the world. President of the successful digital agency Mirum, he also relentlessly blogs, records the weekly podcast "Six Pixels of Separation," writes for the *Harvard Business Review*, and speaks all over the world. With all of that going on, he's also managed to write two books, one of which, *Ctrl Alt Delete*, talks about the need for business to adapt to changing times and for individuals to "reboot who we are and how we work." For real change to happen in life or work, he argues, it has to get personal. We have to get over our laziness, our fear, our trepidation, our unwillingness to experiment: "Here's the truth about your career in a Ctrl Alt Delete world: It's time to stop asking others to convince us about new opportunities (because they're not all that new anymore), and it's time to start doing the hard work of getting things right. For ourselves. For the businesses that we work for. For the industry we serve. For our legacy."

Of course Mitch is not alone in reinventing himself and his career. Richard Branson and Elon Musk and a host of other entrepreneurial geniuses also come to mind.

And while many of these transformations have been pretty dramatic, we think it's important to note that sometimes the shift can be more subtle. All three of us—Ron, Chris and Scott—have reinvented ourselves and our businesses over the years. After years working as a creative director at a traditional ad agency, Ron could see that the marketing landscape was changing. He wanted to work in a new way, with a new approach. So he left to start his own content marketing agency. But he knew that a large part of the challenge in reinventing himself and his business was going to be to change how his clients and those in the business saw him. He didn't want to be pressured to deliver the TV commercials and print ads that he had produced at his old firm. As he puts it:

> *It's your clients who define you in one way. It's your suppliers who define you in one way. It's your colleagues who define you in one way. To truly break free and create a new career and a new agency, I had to break free from all the relationships of my previous life. So I made some promises to myself. I promised myself that I wouldn't partner with anyone I had worked with before. I promised myself that I wouldn't*

hire anyone full-time who I had worked with before. I promised myself that I wouldn't approach any clients I had worked with before. I got new clients. I brought on new partners. I hired new people.

And it worked.

Scott and Chris had much the same experience when they created The Art Of:

We soon realized that part of the reinvention of our business was changing how others saw us. And it was actually our clients who taught us that. We were negotiating speaking engagements with a number of Fortune 500 companies, but we were operating in much the same way we did when we were producing smaller events. A number of our new clients actually had to take us aside and tell us that we simply weren't charging enough for our services. In essence, they told us that if we wanted to play in the big leagues, we had act like big league players. And that made us realize that while we were moving in a new direction, we really hadn't transformed the way we thought of ourselves or our business. And if we hadn't embraced our new identity, neither would our customers.

But it's not just individuals and relatively small operators who can and do embrace reinvention. So do many of the most successful corporate giants. After all, you only have to look at Blockbuster to see the cost of not being willing to change. (We can just imagine the talks around the boardroom table. "Don't worry about Netflix. Everyone *loves* getting in the car on a rainy night and driving out to the strip mall to pick up a DVD. Ordering movies over the Internet—where's the fun in that?")

For the past decade, international research company Millward Brown has been tracking the most valuable global brands through their *BrandZ* study. Their top ten global brands for 2015 were

1. Apple
2. Google
3. Microsoft
4. IBM
5. Visa
6. AT&T
7. Verizon
8. Coca-Cola
9. MacDonald's
10. Marlboro

No surprises here really—with the exception of Marlboro (which always gets a "WTF?" look from audiences when we present this list). But what is interesting is how three of these titans have changed over the years.

Apple

When we think of Apple today, we probably think of iPods, iPads and phones. This company is an entertainment powerhouse that is making money from TV show and movie rentals, music and app purchases, as well has software and hardware sales. Yet it started on April Fool's Day, 1975, as the Apple Computer Company. Apple didn't just keep up with the changing tech world, it reinvented it.

Google

When Larry Page and Sergey Brin met at Stanford in 1995, they started building a search engine called BackRub. (We would like to take this opportunity, on behalf of the whole world, to thank them for ditching the name.) In 1998 they launched Google Inc., and in short order, Google sent most search engines into the scrap yard. The company has also moved far beyond its initial information-gathering focus. Thanks to Google, we are all now thoroughly dependent on Gmail, Google Maps, YouTube, AdWords, Android, Google Chrome and Google+. In 2011, the tech giant acquired Motorola. Google has become more than a brand: it's a verb.

IBM

IBM used to stand for International Business Machines (which always makes us think of those enormous adding machines with the huge handles and the ribbons of paper spewing from the top). Well, they're not really focused on making "business machines" anymore. Now IBM is the world's largest IT and consulting services company.

These three companies have reinvented themselves dramatically, but the truth is that most of the brands on the list have fundamentally changed their business models over time. The best companies continually reinvent themselves, as do many of the most successful people. As Dave Cascino, founder of the innovative group-speaking platform Thunderclap says, "To be successful is to evolve." Dave should know. Two days after he found out that his wife was pregnant, he quit his job to join "StartupBus"—a contest that challenged competitors to develop a company while on the road from San Francisco to Austin. The companies were launched at the SXSW festival. Dave never went back to his job. Instead, he pursued his various ideas and created a new place to work: Thunderclap.

In our careers and our personal lives, reinvention means not allowing yourself to be boxed in by labels or self-imposed definitions. It means moving outside your comfort zone, challenging yourself, being willing to change. Reinventing yourself and the way you think means stopping yourself every time one of these thoughts crosses your mind:

- That's just who I am.
- I can't change.
- This is the way I've always done it.
- This is the way everyone does it.

- This is the way everyone sees it.
- This worked before.
- This is the way I was taught.
- This is what I've always thought.
- This is what I'm comfortable with.
- This is the way it should be done.
- This is the way it has to be done.

To be successful, to solve problems or simply to achieve your goals, think like an artist by being open to new points of view and new experiences, by changing up the way you see things and the way you *do* things.

Go ahead. Be an artist and reinvent your world. But first, start with yourself.

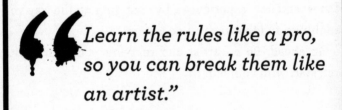

Learn the rules like a pro, so you can break them like an artist."

—Pablo Picasso

BE UNREALISTIC

In Chapter 2, we talked about our issues with the Apple "Crazy Ones" commercial. We expressed concern that it reinforced the conventional thinking that great artists, visionaries and innovators have to be a little crazy. In this chapter, we are fearlessly going to contradict ourselves by saying that all artists *do* have to be a little crazy.

In our defence, by "crazy" we don't really mean wearing a tinfoil hat or believing that reality TV has anything to do with reality. In fact, the craziness we are talking about can be very subtle. It's really more a willingness to be *unrealistic* at times.

The problem many face when trying to solve problems or to come up with new ideas, make improvements in our lives or get ourselves out of self-defeating practices is that we are hedged in by our assumptions of what works, what makes sense, what the reality of our situation looks like. We see only the tried and true way of doing things, the way we've been taught to approach life, the generally accepted perspectives. (Think of all those phrases we mentioned in Chapter 2, the ones that stop you from changing anything.)

Of course, we weren't always this conventional. As we discussed in the first chapter, children tend to have vivid imaginations and an open-minded way of exploring their world. For a child, everything is possible. We were reminded of this while listening to a co-worker talk about her earliest conversation with her younger brother about "careers." He was around four and she was an ancient and world-wise six years old. She asked her brother what he wanted to be when he grew up. "What do you mean?" he said. "Well, if you could be anything. Anything at all," she explained. She was going to go on and give examples: firefighter, teacher, truck driver, when the little boy burst out with, "I know. I want to be an elephant."

Our co-worker was a typical big sister. Which is to say, none too kind. She not only laughed out loud but she also ran to yuk it up with her parents in what was no doubt the start of her little brother's cramped dreams and general disillusionment with life.

Okay, as far as we know, there is still no way to become trans-species, so the kid was never going to realize his dreams. But this is a perfect example of how our imaginations get stifled by rules, conventions and plain old "reality." (Apparently no one in the little boy's world ever suggested he should study mammalogy.) We are told that these are our choices: firefighter, teacher, truck driver. Later, the list might be expanded to sales manager, lawyer, urologist. We are taught the way to wash dishes, do our school work, manage our careers, organize our lives. If we have a particularly type A spouse, we might be told which way the toilet paper roll should be facing. We adopt conventions of thinking about power and politics, financial planning, social structures and household chores. And we largely accept this received wisdom. We become attached to ideas, often without being aware of them. We hang onto thought paradigms even when they cease being useful or have little relationship to reality and our world.

It's not just individuals who do this, but society at large as well. Think about the practice of shaking hands. It actually goes back to at least the fifth century, and is depicted in stone relief carvings from ancient Greece. The gesture is thought to have been a sign of peace. You offer your hand to show that you aren't holding a weapon. Few of us these days are bringing daggers into the boardroom (not literally at least), but it's become a social necessity in the West: try to imagine walking into a meeting or a cocktail party and not shaking hands. People will think you're a Howard-Hughes-calibre germaphobe—or worse.

Some of our favourite examples of our collective attachment to outdated ways of thinking concern food. When cake mixes were widely introduced to the market after the

Second World War, the first formulations required that the baker add nothing other than water. The problem was that most people felt that baking *had to* involve adding together ingredients, plural. They didn't mind taking shortcuts by using a mix, but there was a limit to how short the shortcut could be and still make people feel as if this really was a cake they were making and not wall plaster. The manufacturers changed cake mix formulations so that you had to add water, oil and an egg. Sales took off. Similar prejudices have hampered the sale of any precooked food that is vacuum-sealed in bags. Although vacuum-sealed airtight bags of completely prepared rice, pasta, fish and the like don't need to be refrigerated, there is something about squishy sacs of warm food sitting on a shelf that seem to scream "salmonella!" Most food manufacturers have given up trying to convince people that they are safe, and have gone back to sticking stuff in aluminum cans or containers in the freezer section of the grocery store.

Like most people, you probably aren't aware that you are so attached to orthodox ways of thinking. And while you may have tried to eat Play-Doh or paint a mural with peanut butter when you were imagination-fuelled half-pints, let's be honest, by the time you hit adulthood, you don't experiment much. (Although we do remember seeing a sign in Toronto for the "Creative Driving School." Maybe they meant the mode of instruction was creative, but our first thoughts were that the actual driving was creative. We're all for creativity, but that sounded like a bad idea.)

There's a little activity we sometimes do with groups to illustrate how closely most people stick to the script. It's really simple. Our first step is to ask individuals to write down the name of something they might find in the kitchen.

There is no second step.

We've taken groups through this exercise many times. We've done it with salespeople. Marketing people. Finance people. New hires. Students. We've done it in Canada. The United States. Mexico. It doesn't matter where we do it or whom we do it with, when we say, "Tell us something you'd find in a kitchen," the same things happen. First, many people look a little panicked when we turn to them for their answers. The game seems too easy. They seem to feel there's some mystery item that, when blurted out, initiates a spotlight and a confetti cannon. Or that their faces are instantly going to appear on a big screen looking like stunned winners from Publishers Clearing House. Inevitably, when they respond, they do so cautiously, in the form of a question: "Uh . . . garlic press?"

Of course, there is the other type of person. The ones who love speaking into microphones and hearing the sound of their own voice. They are blurting out their answers even before we've asked.

Most people fall somewhere in between. What almost all people have in common, however, is the type of answer they provide. Responses usually include items like spoon, bread, fridge, stove, microwave, coffee maker, plate, bowl, cup, cereal, blender, butter, can opener, et cetera. In fact, the three most common responses are 1) fork, 2) knife and 3) butter.

Men, women, salespeople, administrators, they all rattle off fork, knife and butter. But while the vast majority of people will offer up kitchen items like these three, there is always one person who breaks from the pack and says something like "a dirty pair of socks." Or "a farting dog."

When those answers are read out, you can see the mood of the group shift. People who have to follow these surprising folks and read out fork, or knife, or butter look a little uncomfortable or sheepish. Even the blurters offer their answers reluctantly, as if they are embarrassed to have come up with such yawn-inducing suggestions. Everyone is wishing that they had thought of the dog or the socks.

But they didn't, because when asked the question, everyone starts to think of the most logical and obvious choices. We all think of things that "should" be in the room, "conventional" kitchen items. Our choices meet everyone's expectations. They are, in other words, "realistic."

Being realistic is safe and risk-free. You are never going to get into trouble with the realistic answer. But it's not going to allow you to be creative in your thinking, or your work either. To do that, you have to move past fork, knife, butter. You have to be imaginative, you have to be unorthodox, you have to be a little *unrealistic*.

Think about the way artists work. The art world is full of examples of visual artists, writers, filmmakers, dancers and so on doing things that others would have thought undoable, unrealistic or just plain nuts if they had heard about them before they were started.

Take Christo and Jeanne-Claude. This couple have now become famous for their highly unusual *temporary* artworks. For *Wrapped Coast*, they literally wrapped 2.5 kilometres of Sydney, Australia's, Little Bay in synthetic fabric. *Surrounded Islands* saw 603,850 square kilometres of ocean waters near Miami covered with pink polypropylene floating fabric. The duo also fabric-wrapped the Pont Neuf in Paris and the Reichstag in Berlin. *The Umbrellas* was an installation of 3,100 six-metre-high blue and yellow umbrellas along valleys in California and Japan, and *The Gates* featured 7,503 frames of vinyl tubing, draped with saffron-coloured fabric, that lined the pathways of New York's Central Park.

Almost everything about this couple's art seems risky and "unrealistic": its enormous scale, its very public nature (they try to build their installations in places that are heavily populated or highly used by people) and, perhaps most strikingly, its ephemeral nature. Many artists would balk at the idea of working on a piece that will literally disappear in a matter of weeks. (Never mind the expense. Christo had to pay $14 million simply to get the *permission* to build his *Over the River* installation in Colorado. A current project in Abu Dhabi, *The Mastaba*, which will become the biggest sculpture in the world, is estimated to cost $350 million—the same amount it would cost if the Eiffel Tower were built today.)

Writing in *Interview* magazine, art historian and critic Barbara Rose describes first meeting Christo and Jeanne-Claude in 1964. She says, "The work they planned to do seemed preposterous in the mid-'60s." Talking to Rose again fifty years later, Christo reinforces that notion. He says that despite the beauty of their work, "It's also absurd."

And yet they embraced this absurdity, creating twenty-two projects over fifty years. But even after they had successfully built installations, garnered admirers and grabbed the attention of the art establishment as well as the general public, their work continued to be "unrealistic." In fact, thirty-seven of their designs were never realized because the couple couldn't get the various permissions to build them. Many of the works they did manage to complete seemed to happen despite the odds. The artists' requests to construct *Wrapped Reichstag* was rejected three times; *Pont Neuf* twice; *The Gates* repeatedly. But Christo and Jeanne-Claude kept on with their unique vision. (With Jeanne-Claude's death in 2009, Christo now continues on his own.)

Of course, Christo and Jeanne-Claude aren't alone in thinking unconventionally.

- Jackson Pollock created his most successful work by throwing paint rather than spreading it with a brush.
- Marina Abramović convinced MOMA to let her do an installation where the general public could

sit across from her and stare for *as long as they wanted.*

- The Beastie Boys decided to create music in the predominantly African-American hip hop world, even though they were three white Jewish kids.
- Frank Lloyd Wright, when commissioned to design a home in a forested river setting, built the house—Fallingwater—with the river running right through it.
- Stand-up comedian Demetri Martin used a flip chart—perhaps the most iconic emblem of deathly boring corporate seminars—to create his hilarious routines.
- Over 230 hours' worth of film was shot for the two-and-a-half-hour movie *Apocalypse Now.*
- Hugely successful solo percussionist Evelyn Glennie creates beautiful music—even though she is deaf.
- Artist Ilana Yahav uses light, sound and *sand* to create art "performances" in front of live audiences.
- Writer and director Richard Linklater filmed his award-winning movie *Boyhood* with the same cast over twelve years.
- Martin Amis wrote a novel, *Time's Arrow*, that moves steadily backward in time.

The list could go on and on.

Artists don't allow themselves to be limited or over-ruled by conventions or received wisdom. Many seem to be following "sound artist" Susan Philipsz's dictum: "Be audacious. . . . It doesn't always have to make sense."

By not being bound by convention, received wisdom or "reality," artists allow their imaginations free rein. They can see what isn't there. And seeing what isn't there means seeing opportunities and possibilities. In that way, a good part of what artists do is, in essence, unrealistic.

One of this book's editors tells the story of another unrealistic artistic endeavour that might easily stand in for any ambitious effort. A good friend had, in her early forties, sold the business management company she had founded in the U.K. in order to try her hand at writing—something she had always wanted to do. Her first foray into this new work was an extensively researched and almost academic book about the divide between working mothers and mothers outside the workforce. Her book got great reviews and plenty of press, but she hungered to switch her focus to fiction. In particular, she thought she would like to write light, humorous novels along the lines of Helen Fielding's Bridget Jones series—as long as she could get them published. She asked our editor what she thought of this new goal. Our editor knew her friend was fiercely intelligent and very talented but had never written any fiction before. And cracking the publishing business, especially with fiction, can be extraordinarily tough. *Are you crazy?* the editor thought. *Do you know how many tens of thousands of people are trying to do that? Do you know that pretty much every one of them is going to be rejected? Do you know that your odds of getting published are only slightly better than your odds of winning the Irish Sweepstakes—without buying a ticket?* But instead of saying any of that, she put her editor hat aside and donned the cap of friendship. "That's great," she said. "Go for it."

After a year and a half had passed, the editor got an email from her friend. The new writer had just been offered a two-book contract by both Random House U.K. and Random House U.S. Her first novel also sold translation rights in at least half a dozen countries. By any publishing standards, this would be like winning the Irish Sweepstakes *and* cleaning up at the craps table in Vegas.

So, being a little "unrealistic" works well when creating works of art and very often in making things happen. The founder of the Humber College School of Creative and Performing Arts, Joe Kertes, provides another good example. Comedian and former Humber College professor Lorne Frohman has described how Joe approached the early days of the school's comedy program. Joe wanted to have some high-wattage comedians do seminars and talks for the first cohort of students, despite the fact that he had no budget. He told Lorne he was thinking of asking Johnny Carson, who had just retired. "He doesn't seem to be doing much," said Joe. "Well," replied Lorne, "I think he planned it that way."

Not to be completely dissuaded by glum reality, Joe moved on to an only slightly less unlikely choice, Chevy Chase. Joe had finagled Chevy's phone number from another Humber staffer who had once worked on *Saturday Night Live*. Much to Lorne's disbelief, Chevy actually returned Joe's call. The two men began to talk about the idea of Chevy doing a guest lecture at Humber. Chevy told Joe his rate for any and all appearances: "My usual fee is $25 million." Joe made a counter-offer: "How about zero?"

There was a moment of silence on the other end of the line. Finally Chevy responded: "You drive a hard bargain."

Chevy showed up at Humber.

That's a story of "don't ask, don't get," but it's also a great testament to the power of taking a risk and being a little unrealistic.

American neurosurgeon Dilan Ellegala knows all about taking risks and being unrealistic. He flew in the face of all conventional medical wisdom when he decided to teach medical officers to perform neurosurgery in a rural African hospital. In his book, *Send Forth the Healing Sun,* journalist Tony Bartelme describes how in 2006 Ellegala accompanied his then-girlfriend to Haydom, Tanzania, where she was starting a six-month residency. Ellegala was planning to take a break from work: he had just finished his own residency in the United States. But he was soon drawn into the hospital wards and found himself performing a number of basic neurosurgeries, often with jerry-rigged equipment. He was troubled both by the incredible surgical need of the community and by the way that visiting doctors, following a long tradition of medical missionary work, would show up at the hospital for a few months, treat a significant number of patients, then return home. When they packed their bags, they left the hospital and the sick Tanzanians as bereft of medical expertise as they had been before the foreigners had arrived. Ellegala decided to change that. He invited a young medical officer, Emmanuel Mayegga, to join him while he performed surgery. Medical officers have some medical training, but they aren't doctors. In Tanzania and in the rest of the international medical world, this would instantly disqualify them from performing any sort of surgery. Surgeons have to be licensed physicians. Neurosurgeons have to complete many extra years of rigorous training and surgical residency.

But Ellegala wondered if it had to be this way. He was sure that the right medical officers—those who were diligent, intelligent and confident—could be taught to do basic neurosurgeries without all of the background training. Sure, it would be better to have the standard education, but there was not enough money or time to train new surgeons if you wanted to make a dint in the African medical landscape in the foreseeable future. And men, women and children were dying because of lack of care. So Ellegala trained Mayegga, and then had Mayegga train another medical officer.

It was an audacious, daring and seemingly unrealistic way to approach the doctor shortage in Haydom. Ellegala was upbraided by a number of practitioners back in the U.S., and was threatened with lawsuits by doctors in Kenya and Tanzania. But he persisted, eventually establishing Madaktari Africa, an NGO that is dedicated to sending surgeons to the developing world to teach surgery to local practitioners rather than simply performing it themselves.

Ellegala's work has greatly contributed to a change of thinking in the international medical community. It has also got a good many people reconsidering the way in which surgeons and other medical specialists are trained in the West. But if Ellegala had surveyed just about anyone—medical expert or not—before he started his work in Africa, he would have been told that his idea was undoable. It was simply *unrealistic*.

The creation of Twitter is another great example of the power of being unrealistic.

We hope we don't have to describe Twitter to you. These days Twitter is so ubiquitous, its use so widespread, that we imagine if you search the term "Twitter," Google responds with, "You're kidding, right?" Since its appearance, Twitter has helped humanity share pointless information, daily ramblings and half-baked opinions, but it has also helped citizens overthrow governments (think Arab Spring). When big stories happen, we turn to Twitter so we can get unbiased news from citizens who are armed with their mobile devices and a desire to report live from the trenches. When live television events like the Oscars or the Super Bowl are broadcast, we complement our experience with the unfiltered grassroots commentary shared by regular schmucks like us on Twitter.

Twitter is amazing. But it wasn't designed to be amazing. Its creators were just patient enough to let it become amazing.

Biz Stone, Jack Dorsey and the team behind Twitter simply wanted to do something interesting with SMS. That's it. It was a side project while they were working on something else. They didn't have whiteboards that mapped out key strategies to recruit 500 million users, integrate promoted tweets, encourage the use of hashtags in TV commercials, or get "Please RT" into everyday language. Although these things didn't cross their mind, they certainly would have shown how "unrealistic" this venture really was. It was, after all, just a bunch of people following a quirky idea—with no greater purpose than the challenge of creating something new and unique.

Even the name of the app was not chosen in a way that took into account what might work in the "real world." Noah Glass had generated a few names but was trying to convince the team to go with "Jitter." He had also come up with "Twitter." All of the names were put into a draw, and when the latter was pulled out, Biz pushed for it. Biz's wife is a wildlife rehabilitation specialist and a birder, so he knew that "Twitter" meant short bursts of song used by birds to communicate. (Had he not known that one trivial fact, we would probably be following people on "Jitter" and instead of retweets, we'd be saying something like "Jit-Jit." You wouldn't be a tweeter, you'd be an "ijit.")

"If we had done market tests on the name, it never would

have been approved," Biz told an audience at The Art of Marketing a number of years ago. "It was an easy choice because we were only three people. Had there been more chefs in the kitchen, we would have probably ended up calling it something like 'Microblogger.' It literally came out of names in a hat, and we were small enough to just go with it. But we also didn't think it would ever work. I said, 'Ultimately, it doesn't even matter. It's not going to work anyways.'"

We will come back later in the book to talk about how the Twitter team handled their early doubters and critics, but what we like about the Twitter genesis story is that it so clearly shows the value of pursuing ideas, even if they don't make sense on traditional balance sheets. Artists aren't afraid of working on ideas or projects that don't always seem to be realistic or reasonable and neither are many of our most innovative companies and business people.

Scooter Braun, the talent manager behind Justin Bieber, Psy, Carly Rae Jepsen, The Wanted, Ariana Grande and other performers, has obviously been tremendously successful. And not just in marketing musicians. He's also branched out to movies, TV and other investments, like the music-streaming service Songza and Uber.

We interviewed Scooter at The Art of Marketing in Vancouver in September 2013, asking him about his approach to entrepreneurialism and his thoughts on marketing a person as a brand. How does he approach it? What is his philosophy? What are the reasons behind his success? What was most important? What was least important? Where did he make more money? Where? Why? How? He summarized his thoughts with advice that really stuck with us: "You have to be unrealistic."

Allowing ourselves, as individuals or as members of an organization, to be "unrealistic" can clearly have great benefits.

While many entrepreneurs have benefited from the ability to embrace what appears to be unrealistic at first, former COO and business speaker Cameron Herold has developed two business approaches that can make being unrealistic part of the corporate culture. Described in his book *Double Double*, "Vivid Vision" is a strategy in which CEOs and corporate leaders "lean out" three years into the future and imagine what their company might look like.

When we spoke to him recently, Cameron told us, "They describe every aspect of their company as if they're standing and walking around their businesses. They describe marketing and IT and operations and engineering. They describe the meeting rhythms and the corporate culture. They write down what the customers are saying and what their interactions are like with the company. They put down what the media is writing about them." Cameron notes that while the executives are describing the desired future state of their company as fully as they can, they have to imagine that they have gone into a time machine and arrived at a future date. In other words, they don't know how they got where they are—and they aren't trying to figure that out. After the leadership team has written up this "vivid vision" (usually a four-page document), they present it to the rest of the company and say, "This is what our future looks like. Let's figure out how to make it happen."

The next step, getting everyone to think more creatively about the way forward, is what Cameron calls the "Can You Imagine Wall." In his early days as COO of 1-800-GOT-JUNK?, he and CEO and founder Brian Scudamore were talking about what they might do to get everyone in their company excited and dreaming about the future the way they were dreaming. They happened to be standing in the lobby as they talked, in front of a large blank wall. That's when it occurred to them that the empty space, the first thing everyone—employees, customers and suppliers—saw when they walked into the building would be a great place to share ideas. Crazy, ambitious, imaginative ideas. The "Can You Imagine Wall" was born. The first two "unrealistic" suggestions that went up were "Can you imagine having 100 franchises?" (They had twenty at the time.) And "Can you imagine being featured on *Oprah*?" Both were realized. (1-800-GOT-JUNK? now has hundreds of locations in Canada, Australia and the U.S.) So too was becoming a case study in Harvard's MBA program and appearing on the sides of five million Starbucks cups.

When Cameron now describes his "Can You Imagine Wall" strategy to business executives, he suggests that the leadership team encourage suggestions from employees, suppliers and customers. The team should then select ideas—even if they seem pretty out there—that line up with their own "vivid vision." Those one-sentence ideas are then put up on a wall in a public space (a lobby, a large meeting room or the lunchroom)—with the name of the person who suggested them. A checkmark is then placed next to each idea as it is realized.

Cameron notes that one of the reasons the "Vivid Vision" and "Can You Imagine" techniques are so powerful is that they encourage people to turn private ideas public. He has noticed that once people commit an idea to paper, once they start sharing it with people, they seem to feel a commitment to making it happen. What's more, he says, "People are going to begin to conspire to help you make it come true; they'll work towards it too." Turns out that people get pretty excited about the idea of making "crazy" ideas come to life.

But what is it about a dash of unrealism that is so magical? Let's get back to that fork, knife, butter exercise.

After we have asked everyone to read out their kitchen items, we proceed to the next step in the activity. (Okay, we lied. There is a Step 2.) We ask the group, "What was the most memorable item mentioned?"

You know what people *don't* say? Fork. Knife. Or butter.

Not only do people not say these words, they've *never* said them. Even though fork, knife and butter are mentioned almost every time, none has ever been chosen as the most memorable item. *Ever*.

The ones the group does choose as the most memorable are the fun items. The creative. The unique. The funny. The odd. As Christo has said about his own work, "People like . . . to see something totally irrational, totally useless in some ways." Artists create something new and different. And people like new and different. Even in the kitchen.

All very well and good, you may be thinking. *But I'm a fork person through and through. How I am going to come up with the equivalent of "farting dog" next time a creative answer is called for?*

In Chapter 1, we talked a bit about what creative thinking is and how it happens. And in the next two chapters, we will talk about a number of ways that artists access their creativity and come up with ideas. But here it is worth discussing one of the ways people have been trying to stretch their creative muscles for the last several decades: brainstorming.

Brainstorming was developed at the end of the 1940s by BBDO ad man Alex Osborn. He thought that the only way for American businesses to thrive and to be competitive on an international stage was to be more creative. He began to turn his focus from the ad world to helping business people develop their creative thinking. In 1942 he published the book *How to Think Up*, which introduced the idea of brainstorming, followed in 1948 by *Your Creative Power*, which included the chapter "How to Organize a Squad to Create Ideas." His idea was that people should join together to generate as many ideas as possible in a relatively short period of time. In order not the quash what he called the "delicate flower" of creativity, a brainstorming session was to allow no negative reactions—feedback and critiques could only be offered if they were positive. But response was not really the point of the exercise, nor was quality—

the group's goal was to come up with a significant *quantity* of ideas. The objective was to allow the imagination to run free, to park conventional thinking at the door, to allow a little "unrealism" into the room. It was like the advice that architect Sunand Prasad gives to anyone trying be more creative: "Once there's an idea, turn it upside down and take it seriously for a moment—even if it seems silly." The farting-dog guy would be in his element.

Osborn's approach became hugely popular. The term *brainstorming* entered the lexicon (updated slightly to *blue-sky thinking* in some circles), and meeting rooms across the globe became home to flip charts and markers as well as stale coffee and dry muffins.

While brainstorming sessions were sometimes helpful, the problem with the traditional model is that it doesn't really work that well, as neuropsychologist Jonah Lehrer touched on in his *New Yorker* article "GroupThink."

Lehrer notes that a Yale University study done in 1958 showed that when asked to generate new ideas, individuals came up with about twice as many—and better—ideas than those working in groups. This may be explained in part by a 2011 Texas A&M University study ("Collaborative Fixation: Effects of Others' Ideas on Brainstorming" in *Applied Cognitive Psychology*) that showed that group-brainstorming activities seemed to result in members focusing on a few ideas that had already been presented, often generating subsequent ideas that were merely derivative of the ones that had caught people's attention. In other words, the sharing the group was doing was inhibiting creative thinking and new ideas instead of facilitating them.

So should we ditch the idea of brainstorming altogether if we want people to think more creatively? Not at all.

Alex Osborn was onto something when he suggested that people—everyone, not just artists and creative types—should be allowed to let their imaginations go. His focus, however, was the business team, and he was concerned about co-workers quashing each other's creative impulses. And while all of us know people who treat new ideas like they were Ebola, most of us who are painting our walls a tasteful "greige" and taking the same vacation we took last year know that it's not *other* people who are stomping on our little flashes of craziness—it's us. We have a little inner censor who is busy blacklining anything that seems new, unusual, risky or unrealistic. But if we want to think and work more creatively, we absolutely need to shut the guy up. (More on this in Chapter 8.)

No, it's not the unfettered idea-generation part of brainstorming that doesn't really work. It's the idea of doing it in a group setting—asking people to come up with ideas when they are sitting next to their boss and the young new hire who really wants their job. It's asking people to think for themselves when everything they hear sounds better than whatever they thought of.

In fact, when the group-brainstorming set-up is altered slightly, the generation of quality ideas vastly improves. The key seems to be allowing individuals to come up with ideas on their own, in private, then pool the ideas with the group before going back to private mulling. And if the group sharing session allows debate, if people challenge some of the ideas presented and discuss weaknesses as well as strengths, the second round of idea generation produces many more new, strong ideas. In other words, sharing ideas with other people can really encourage creative thinking— as long as there is space for individuals to engage in this thinking on their own time and in their own space.

If we look at the way artists think and work, this should really be no surprise.

The stereotype of the artist is the solitary figure, suffering alone in a cold garret. And it is true that most artists work alone. But as the Christo and Jeanne-Claude example proves, not all do. In fact, a lot of artistic endeavours are dependent on partnerships and group work. For example, if I ask you to come up with the names of song-writing teams, you may have a hard time finding an end to the list: Gilbert and Sullivan, Rodgers and Hammerstein, Ira and George Gershwin, Burt Bacharach and Hal David, Hayes and Porter, Lennon and McCartney, Simon and Garfunkel, Jagger and Richards, Ashford and Simpson, Elton John and Bernie Taupin, Jerry Garcia and Robert Hunter, Don Henley and Glenn Frey, Joe Strummer and Mick Jones, Bono and the Edge, Timbaland and Missy Elliott, André 3000 and Big Boi, Killer Mike and El-P.... Okay, okay, we're just going to have to stop. (And we didn't even get into the bands who write music in true multi-member collaboration.)

While there are fewer examples of writing teams in the realm of literary fiction, the examples of creative teams writing for television and film are as many as those of the music world. And of course actors and dancers are almost always practising their art in collaboration with others—whether it's their directors and choreographers or fellow cast members and performers.

And then there are the comedy troupes. In his biography, *So, Anyway . . .*, and in various interviews over the last few years, Monty Python alumnus John Cleese has described the creative power of working with others, particularly in a group in which the members have different strengths. In an interview with the *Harvard Business Review*, he noted, "Traditionally, comedy writers have worked in pairs, and I like that. I do believe that when you collaborate with someone else on something creative, you get to places that you would never get to on your own. The way an idea builds as it careens back and forth between good writers is so unpredictable. Sometimes it depends on people misunderstanding each other, and that's why I don't think there's any such thing as a mistake in the creative process. You never know where it might lead."

Even when poets, painters, photographers, sculptors, performance artists and so on are working solo, they often gravitate to others who work in their medium or even with other forms of art. No doubt this is in part because they need to get a reprieve from those of us lunkheads who don't always understand what they are doing, or how they are doing it, but it's no doubt also a way for them to exchange ideas, get inspiration, challenge others and be challenged. Think, for example, of the 1920s Algonquin Round Table, that collection of writers, actors, humourists and critics—Dorothy Parker, Robert Benchley, George S. Kaufman, Harold Ross, to name a few—who gathered regularly at New York City's famous Algonquin Hotel to discuss and debate, to exchange stories and witty retorts, and to get quietly, and not so quietly, trashed. The Bloomsbury Group, whose most famous members included E. M. Forster, Duncan Grant, Vanessa and Clive Bell, Virginia and Leonard Woolf, was a similar gathering of artists, art critics and writers (and one economist—John Maynard Keynes, how did you sneak in there?) who met to exchange ideas, engage in intellectual debate and support each other.

The nineteenth-century Impressionist painters—Claude Monet, Édouard Manet, Paul Cézanne and Camille Pissarro among others—famously gathered together to share their art, hold exhibits and support each other when the French Académie des Beaux-Arts closed its doors—and its collective mind—to their new and iconoclastic approach to painting. In Canada, our Group of Seven painters, sharing a similar yet individually distinctive approach to capturing the Canadian landscape, not only challenged and encouraged each other's creativity, but showed work together and helped all members capture the attention of the art world. In short, while creativity may blossom when people work alone, it is often kept alive when it is shared with others who appreciate its uniqueness, its difference and its embrace of the unrealistic.

Interestingly, there seems to be a growing amount of evidence that creativity is also fostered by the exchange of ideas with others who do not share the same interests or expertise. Steve Jobs famously built the Pixar office complex to force employees from different departments to mingle with each other. He refused to put the offices of accountants next to the offices of other accountants, in favour of mixing up finance people, tech experts, animators, writers, HR folk and so on. He created a floor plan that funnelled everyone into the lobby concourse, even initially putting the only washrooms in the shared area. He initiated a seminar series that was open to every employee. What he suspected and was soon confirmed by Pixar's extraordinarily successful output was that organic casual conversations between people with different talents and focuses ignited new thoughts, generated novel ideas and boosted everyone's creativity. This "campus" work environment has been recreated by a host of tech companies and many other organizations that are committed to creative thinking. In other words, companies are wanting workers to spend more time rather than less chatting around the water cooler.

So back to the idea of being a bit unrealistic. If we want to think more creatively, we need to follow the artists' lead and allow ourselves to generate "unrealistic" ideas, embrace "unrealistic" ways of doing or thinking. But being a little unorthodox doesn't mean that we shouldn't challenge and hone our ideas and our thinking, and work to help them reach their potential, whatever that might be. (In fact, you have to look no further than to reality shows like *So You Think You Can Dance* and *American Idol* to see what happens when we skip this last step. The first episodes of those talent searches always go for laughs by showcasing hapless shoe store clerks warbling painfully off key, or sweaty, nervous bundles of elbows and knees skidding around on the dance floor, showing off their moves. Pure, unimproved creative effort, in other words.) Artists like Christo and Jeanne-Claude make the unrealistic work. They do this by meeting the many challenges they are presented with, by thinking through every step in the designs, by finding ways to maintain the magic, the imagination, in the practical world. They come up with inspiration, and then they refine that inspiration.

So, go ahead. Walk away from conventional thinking and the way you—and others—have always done things. Come up with your craziest ideas. Then challenge yourself to improve on these ideas, generate better ones or refine the ones you have. Make these new ideas workable for you. This might mean putting your work and ideas aside for a time and revisiting them with a fresh eye. Or it may mean sharing them with a trusted colleague or group and responding to their feedback.

And if you are having trouble coming up with those ideas in the first place, you may need to stop, look and listen.

A piece of art is never a finished work. It answers a question which has been asked, and asks a new question."

—Robert Engman, sculptor

STOP, LOOK AND LISTEN

R on Tite, one of the authors of this book, was raised on country music. Not, he sheepishly admits, the hip alt-country variety either. The good old-fashioned, cryin'-in-your-beer, grammatically challenged kind. So when we sat down to make notes about this chapter, Ron couldn't help himself. He started spouting the lyrics from one of his mother's favourite Patsy Cline tunes, "Stop, Look and Listen" (which you have to admit is a really great song). Patsy sings about a "cool cat" who lives fast and is going to "run outta gas." She tells anyone else who is acting like this that they better stop, look and listen because they might end up "missin' kissin'."

This song was written in the 1950s, so there's a good chance that "living fast" would look like an episode of

SpongeBob SquarePants by today's standards. Regardless, Patsy's song can be seen as a holistic and inspirational "stop and smell the roses" (or "don't be missin' kissin'") kind of message. And its homespun advice is now more important than ever.

Stopping to enjoy life is one thing, but with the tsunami of information and technological change that hits our shores these days, we have to stop just so we can know what the heck's going on. (Ron Tite just noticed that he had forty-six app updates waiting to be initiated on his phone. And it's not as if he hasn't hit the "update all" button since the early '90s.) Patsy's right. We don't know what we're missing out on because there's so much being generated that we can't keep up. Our heads are buried in our hand-helds and laptops, and we hardly have time to think, never mind think creatively.

We all know the effect this tsunami is having. You'd love to develop a new sales approach, but you have to catch up on all those great Mashable articles you haven't gotten to yet. You'd love to redesign your kitchen, but it looks like a brilliant young mind has just uploaded a TED video you just have to see. You'd love to rethink your career, but there's a new white paper on compensation that you'd like to read first. And on and on.

How is the creativity supposed to come out of those scenarios? If artists acted like we act, they'd never have an original thought in their lives. Most artists, however, recognize that quiet contemplation and time alone with their thoughts, while it may look to others like inactivity, is an essential part of what they do.

Reading *Daily Rituals: How Artists Work*, by Mason Currey (an entertaining look at the quotidian routines of great artists and thinkers), we were struck by how many of these fascinating, creative people shared the same pastime. *Off-track betting?* you are wondering. *Illicit love affairs? Maybe a little recreational drug use?* No, nothing as edgy or potentially illegal as that. It was *walking*. Just plain old walking.

Yes, Gustav Mahler, Wallace Stevens, Benjamin Britten, Georgia O'Keeffe, Charles Dickens, Sergei Rachmaninoff, Vladimir Nabokov, Pyotr Ilyich Tchaikovsky, Søren Kierkegaard and Alice Munro, among others, all made a point of taking a lengthy daily walk. Many acknowledged the importance of this quiet time to their work. Charles Dickens walked for three hours a day, thinking about what he was writing, "searching for some pictures I wanted to build upon." Currey describes Tchaikovsky's perambulations: "His walks were essential to his creativity, and he often stopped to jot down ideas that he would later flesh out at the piano."

Contemporary playwright Polly Stenham is part of this walking club and says to all aspiring artists: "Go for a walk. Every morning I go to Hampstead Heath [in north London], and I often also go for a wander in the middle of the day to think through a character or situation."

Walking is the way that these artists "stop," as Patsy says. Of course, it isn't the only way. Musician Guy Garvey initially found his quiet time in a pew: "Spending time in your own head is important. When I was a boy, I had to go to church every Sunday; the priest had an incomprehensible Irish accent, so I'd tune out for the whole hour, just spending time in my own thoughts. I still do that now; I'm often scribbling down fragments that later act like trigger-points for lyrics." Walking is such a common spur to creativity because it's one of the things that most people never stop doing—even if it's only in shamefully short bursts for some of us.

However we manage it, for most people, creativity and creative thinking are dependent on *time*—time alone, time without interruptions, time without a million tasks and a to-do list hovering before our eyes.

Okay, great, you're probably thinking. *But I'm a busy gal.* The irony is that, for most of us, finding quiet time takes some creativity itself, as well as considerable planning and significant discipline. That's especially true if you work for any sort of big organization. If you are on that kind of treadmill you know about the back-to-back meetings, the conference calls, the report writing, the report reading, the number crunching, the charity events. There's always one more thing to do before you can stop to breathe. One more email. One more spreadsheet. One more phone call. And for those who leave the office—or any workplace—for the "second shift" of the day, there is also one more pickup at school, one more soccer practice to get to, one more dinner to cook, one more load of laundry to put in before you can collapse into bed.

For many of us, it seems that quiet time has to wait another day. Or does it? Writing in the *Harvard Business Review*, Freek Vermeulen, associate professor of strategy and entrepreneurship at the London Business School, points out that many business giants see "stopping" as part of the job:

The CEO of a large, global bank once told me: "It is very easy for someone in my position to be very busy all the time. There is always another meeting you really have to attend, and you can fly some-where else pretty much every other day. However, I feel that that is not what I am paid to do. It is my job to carefully think about our strategy."

I believe his view is spot-on. And there are other successful business leaders who understand the value of making time to think. Bill Gates, for example, was famous for taking a week off twice a year—spent in a secret waterfront cottage—just to think and reflect deeply about Microsoft and its future without any interruption. Similarly, Warren Buffett has said, "I insist on a lot of time being spent, almost every day, to just sit and think."

If you can't find time to think, it probably means that you haven't organized your firm, unit, or team very well, and you are busy putting out little fires all the time. It also means that you are at risk of leading your company astray.

Stopping is not an excuse to be lazy. It can be a way to be much more productive. Let's be honest with ourselves. Our ability to stop is dictated only by our ability to work stopping into our schedule. There are a number of ways we can do that.

It might mean turning something that you have to do anyhow into quiet, device-free, solitary intervals. Some people find that they do their best thinking during long showers, grocery shopping or while doing housework. Time at the gym, running, biking and so on may also give you the opportunity to be alone with your thoughts. (If you are the type who silently sings along with the music, however, you might want to leave your iPod at home.) Walking to work, if you are lucky enough to live close by, is an obvious choice. Taking public transportation instead of driving can be another good option.

One mid-level executive we know takes the streetcar every day, even though she has a car and there is parking at her office. What's more, she's opted for the streetcar over the subway because it gives her a longer break: "The subway only takes me thirty minutes or so, but I have to change lines midway through. But there's a streetcar I can get at the end of my street. It takes me forty-five minutes, but I don't have to do anything but sit there. Sometimes I read, sometimes I do a little paperwork, but mostly I try to spend that time thinking about problems I am struggling with at work or ideas for new projects. I keep a pen and paper handy. On the return trip home, it's my time to catch up on reading and to decompress." The key to making your commute a creative time is to close the newspaper, put down the tablet and spend the time thinking.

If you are the kind of person who is disciplined—and hungry—enough to take lunch breaks, you might change up how you spend them. Try going for a solitary walk at lunch a few times a week instead of grabbing sushi with your co-workers.

Our favourite approach to finding time, however, is to actually "book it." One sales director we know has booked, in his company's shared corporate calendar, a weekly two-hour business review with a colleague. Both of these hardworking guys know that the phone meetings are never going to happen. It's their way of having a block of time, at least once a week, during which other co-workers are not going to call them or book them for a meeting. For one of them, this is an opportunity to have some quiet thinking and working time. The other has been known to occasionally spend his allotment destressing at the local skating rink.

But you don't have to involve anyone else in this booking-time strategy. With your electronic calendar system, you can send yourself a meeting request and then accept it, so that it goes in your schedule. If someone else is helping to manage your time (whether it's your executive assistant or your spouse), tell that person not to cancel or move that appointment. Treat it like it was a meeting with your most important client. Because it is. This is the time when you can focus on creative problem solving or on developing new products, projects or business strategies. You might be doing a little private brainstorming, or even heading out to experience a competitor's product, experience innovation in another sector or simply people-watch to see what ideas that might generate.

Another one of our favourite ways to carve out a little thinking time is to take advantage of the work disruptions that come with business travel. At lot of people treat business travel like the flu—something to get over as quickly as possible. We've seen people sprint from a client's boardroom to catch an early flight just as the last syllable of "thank you for coming" is leaving their host's lips. But is such haste always necessary? Why not *stop* and linger for a while?

One young engineer, beginning to travel for work for the first time, described a site inspection he and a colleague had to do in a small town a few hours outside of Saskatoon. "It was great," he said. "There was only one flight in and one flight out of Saskatoon that worked for us. That meant we had to arrive during the afternoon the day before and leave the following evening, and the inspection only took an hour." So, despite the drive to the little town, there was a lot of down time. The two spent some of that working remotely, but they also used the hotel gym and walked the streets of Saskatoon for an hour or two. It was quiet time that the young engineer seldom gets during his regular weekly routine. "I was able to spend some time thinking about new things I wanted to try with our modelling program. And I actually came back to the office feeling refreshed and energized," he said.

Stopping and spending some time in the places you travel can give you a little mental space, and taking time to check out the town and local life can also help you understand your clients, colleagues and competition. So next time you're on a business trip, try not to dash to the airport like you're going into labour.

While it is often up to the individual to carve out the time to stop, if you are the boss, you can create an entire "culture of stopping" by encouraging or mandating others to stop as well. Google famously gives engineers "20% time," during which they can drop what they are working on to focus on personal projects. (This practice of personal thinking time on the job was actually started decades ago by innovation giant 3M.) It seems to be effective. After Google produced Gmail, AdSense and Google News, it's not surprising that a lot of other companies developed similar "personal time" programs. Apple launched "Blue Sky," LinkedIn launched "Incubator," and Microsoft launched the "Garage." They all seemed to recognize that you can't look to the future with your head buried in today.

Of course, the first big challenge to stopping is finding or creating the time to stop. The second, perhaps equally tough, hurdle is clearing the mental space. You're not going to come up with brilliant new ideas while out for a jog if there is a little voice in your head reciting tomorrow's to-do list. Nor is your imagination going to run free if your inner Excel sheet is busy totting up year-end sales.

In Chapter 1, we talked about the apparent usefulness of daydreaming or letting the mind wander. But you may have noticed that in describing what they did on their daily walks, artists talked about thinking about their work. Yet it seems important that they were doing this in a space where they couldn't actually *do* this work. Where their bodies were occupied by something other than work, while their minds were mulling. Being absent from their homes and offices also probably meant that they were not thinking about dishes to be done or bills to be paid. Rex Jung, the neuropsychologist we met in Chapter 1, argues for the need for this creative mental space. He notes that silencing our more pedestrian thoughts is necessary to access and strengthen at least one aspect of our creativity—"the ability to imagine reality in time and space with no external representation . . . to visualize, imagine, and think of things that aren't literally in front of your eyes." What he refers to as "imaginability."

In an interview for the *Atlantic*, Jung explains: "Most creative people stumble upon their tool to increase their imaginability, whether it's taking a bath or a walk or a drink of bourbon. They find some way to turn down the noise of the conscious mind so ideas can flow more naturally. People may prefer to meditate, exercise, or just lay in bed all day, but they have to know themselves and how their minds work before tapping into their creativity systematically." He goes on to point out that knowing how your mind works can take time itself, and should really start in childhood—which is why he advocates for maintaining recess breaks and downtime for kids.

Minor distractions, like walking, seem to help some of us follow Dr. Jung's advice and turn down the racket in our conscious minds. But there are other ways. Ravi Mehta, a business professor at the University of Illinois, and his research team have studied ambient sound levels and how they affect creative problem solving. They asked subjects to work at alternate-uses tasks in a quiet environment (50 decibels and less); a moderately noisy one (70 dB), and a very noisy one (85 dB). To give you an idea of what those levels mean, 50 dB might be the noise level in a home in a quiet suburban neighbourhood; 70 dB is the level of a vacuum cleaner; 85 dB is like running the garbage disposal or making a smoothie in a blender. Perhaps not surprisingly, the subjects showed their poorest performances in the loudest workplaces. But their strongest performances were in moderate-noise environments, not quiet ones. It seems that a moderately noisy spot—like a crowded coffee shop—provides just enough distraction to allow people to let go of a tightly focused pattern of thought and think more creatively. (It's interesting to note that the researchers looked not only at how the subjects did on creative tasks but also at how open they were to adopting innovative products. Those "shopping" in the mid-range noise were more interested in the innovative items. Now you know why you can't buy a pair of pants without being serenaded by Top 40 hits.)

Some people find that even bigger distractions help them get into a creative headspace. One writer we know finds that turning the TV on helps overcome writer's block. As long as the show is fairly mindless (she finds reality TV or police procedurals work particularly well), she can start jotting down ideas during the commercial breaks or during the slow bits of the show. Writing this way makes her feel that she isn't really working and keeps her from feeling inhibited by her "internal editor," the voice in her head that tells her everything she is writing is crap. Before she knows it, she is thoroughly engrossed in what's she writing and is only vaguely aware of some annoying noise in the background. Then she can snap off the TV and continue.

Some psychologists suggest that keeping a few toys on your desk can help free your mind in a similar fashion. A Rubik's Cube or a small model, for example, can distract that part of your brain that might be tempted to search the Internet for a shoe sale or click on that article about the European Union. With thoughts of cross-trainers and euros pushed aside by a little piece of plastic that doesn't want to fit into the damn place it's supposed to fit, the rest of your mind is free to explore your own, more interesting, thoughts and ideas. Perhaps even more importantly, the toys keep your hands busy and away from the keyboard.

Playwright Polly Stenham says that during her daily walks, she also embraces mild distraction: "I listen to music as I go. Again, it's about occupying one part of your brain, so that the other part is clear to be creative."

Okay, so that's the "stop" part of Patsy Cline's message. But what about the "look and listen"? Stopping and taking a step back can give you the breather you might need to refresh your thinking, re-energize your imagination and make space for some new ideas. But quiet time isn't usually enough on its own to get the creative juices flowing. You also need to find the sparks that ignite new ideas. For most artists, those sparks come from keen observation.

To state the obvious, what we think of as "realistic" visual art is based on observation. Indeed Renaissance art was marked by the movement away from the symbolic representation of medieval painting and sculpture to that based on intense scrutiny (and lessons from ancient Greek and Roman artists). It features realistic proportions in the human body, an accurate portrayal of the way light falls on subjects, and perspective to create a sense of depth—all dependent on careful observation.

But the way looking and listening contribute to art and to creativity does not have to be so literal. (And obviously not all great art is realistic.) For example, singer-songwriter Martha Wainwright describes how an act as simple as looking out the window can provide her with ideas for her songs: "The little images that I get from sitting alone in my apartment—the way the light is falling through the window; the man I just saw walk by on the other side of the street—find their way into snatches of lyrics."

Other composers have used what they have seen and what they have heard to create music: Felix Mendelssohn was so enchanted with the sound of the waves and the echoes of a coastal cave on a boat trip along the Scottish coast that he wrote his *Hebrides Overture (Fingal's Cave)* to capture it. Vivaldi's *Four Seasons* mimics sounds that he heard throughout the year: barking dogs and birdsongs, summer thunderstorms and icy winds.

The important thing to note about observation is that being selective about what you are taking in defeats the purpose of "looking and listening." For one thing, if you think you know what you are looking for, that's what you're likely to notice. It's like the conventional thinking we talked about in Chapter 3. You are going to see what you expect to see, hear what you expect to hear. Or you are going to be so focused on the one thing that you've decided deserves your attention that you are not going to see what else is going on.

Don't believe us? Try this little test. Go to YouTube and search for "Monkey Business Illusion Test" or "Selective Attention Test." Follow the instructions. We'll wait.

For those who didn't do the test, in the video there are two groups of people in close range—one group in white shirts, one in black. They are passing a basketball back and forth. Your instruction, before watching the video, is to count how many passes the white group makes.

How many of you who watched the video counted fifteen? How many of you who were counting noticed the man in the gorilla costume walk through the scene? The test was designed by research psychologists Christopher Chabris and Daniel Simons to examine how people's attention works. Among most viewers, 50 per cent don't even notice the gorilla. They're just so focused on what they feel is important that they tune out everything else. (Chabris and Simon's book on attention, perception, memory and reasoning, *The Invisible Gorilla*, was published in 2010.)

Being truly open to observing what is going on around you may mean stopping yourself from focusing and selecting so that the scope and the significance of what you see and hear are broadened. By doing so, you are going to take more away from your observations. In other words, you can't always know what you're looking for.

Photographer Bill Cunningham provides a great illustration of the way in which artists, through their ability to look and listen more carefully than most, create inspired works of art. Recently featured in the documentary *Bill Cunningham New York*, he has been shooting fashion for the *New York Times* for many years. His two pages, "Evening Hours" and "On the Street," are filled with photos of real and unsuspecting New Yorkers wearing the clothes they picked out from their closet that morning. That's it. It's street style in the purest sense. He's catching humans in their most basic and natural habitat: reluctantly trudging off to work in the morning thinking about the day that lies ahead. In doing so, he lets everyday New Yorkers tell him, and the fashion world, what's hot, and he highlights trends that neither his subjects nor clothing designers may even be aware of. "I let the street speak to me," Cunningham says. "In order for the street to speak to you, you've got to stay out there and see what it is . . . You have to stay on the street and let the street tell you what it is."

Bill Cunningham is the ultimate observer. By staying completely outside of the fashion world, he has a hand in shaping it. He stops. He looks. He listens. As a result, he's often ahead of those who are on the inside. Anna Wintour, editor-in-chief of *Vogue* magazine, has said of Bill's art and his influence, "He and I and all of my team and all the rest of the world, we're sitting in the same fashion shows but he sees something on the street or on the runway that completely missed all of us and in six months time, you know, that will be a trend."

Actors are another group of artists whose craft is dependent on keen observation. More than a few *People* magazine profiles have been about actors who immerse themselves in the world of the character they are about to portray before filming shoots. Renée Zellweger went to work in a London office for several weeks before playing Bridget Jones. Robert De Niro drove a cab for several weeks before filming *Taxi Driver* and set up residence in Sicily, soaking up southern Italian life before starring in *The Godfather Part II.* Charlize Theron spent time with serial killer Aileen Wuornos, observing her physical movements and speech patterns before portraying her in *Monster*.

Other actors use their observations of the world around them to inspire their work in a different way. In a recent *Time* magazine interview, *Orphan Black* actor Tatiana Maslany explains that one of the techniques she uses to make each of the almost a dozen clones she portrays instantly recognizable and distinct is observing and mimicking the physical movements of different animals. "When I first started working with Alison [an uptight soccer-mom clone], it was a lot of work with the idea of a bird—the way a bird moves, how a bird might hold their body up. It became something that was then subconscious. I wasn't thinking about being a bird or whatever, just using that physicality to inspire me differently." (Fans of the show might like this tidbit: for the clone Sarah, Maslany has used the movements of a lion or a rat.)

Sharp observation of people and the world around them is also the basis of many comedians' work. Jerry Seinfeld is the king of this type of humour. The most financially successful stand-up of all time, Seinfeld's supremacy is interesting considering that he can't really act, he's not that animated, he doesn't do impressions, and he has no props or gimmicks. What he does have, however, is X-ray vision and bat-like hearing when it comes to the world around him. And while he may see the same things the rest of us see, what he notices about all of it is the absurd, wacky and nonsensical, whether it has to do with airline peanuts, jobs, dating, horse racing, laundry or painkillers.

Installation artist and filmmaker Isaac Julien seemingly pays attention to just about everything too. "I have a magpie attitude to inspiration," he says.

> *I seek it from all sorts of sources; anything that allows me to think about how culture comes together. I'm always on the lookout—I observe people in the street; I watch films, I read, I think about the conversations that I have. I consider the gestures people use, or the colours they're wearing. It's about taking all the little everyday things and observing them with a critical eye; building up a scrapbook which you can draw on. Sometimes, too, I look at other artworks or films to get an idea of what not to do.*

Most of us aren't that attentive (or we see what we expect to see). But we should be. Dr. John Semple, the visual artist turned neurosurgeon we met in the Introduction, singles out attentiveness when explaining how being an artist has helped him be a better neurosurgeon: "A training in art is really a training in observation. It teaches you how to be aware and how to see. And that's certainly something you can use extremely well in medicine."

Nirmal Joshi, chief medical officer of Pennsylvania-based Pinnacle Health System, would probably agree with Dr. Semple. Writing in the *New York Times* ("Doctor, Shut Up and Listen"), he suggests that much suboptimal medical treatment arises from the fact that doctors are simply not paying attention. "On average," he notes, "physicians wait just 18 seconds before interrupting patients' narratives of their symptoms." In fact, he writes, "A review of reports by the Joint Commission, a non-profit that provides accreditation to health organizations, found that communication failure (rather than a provider's lack of technical skill) was at the root of over 70 per cent of serious adverse health outcomes in hospitals." Recognizing the importance of "soft skills" in medicine, Dr. Joshi and his colleagues have started a program to help physicians improve their communication with patients.

Listening can be hugely important in the business world too. Today, a lot of brands and companies are using social media channels to raise awareness of their products and services and get their messages out. Some also use social media to get feedback and avert PR disasters.

The sorry tale of the new Gap logo isn't exactly a story of an averted PR disaster, but it is a great illustration of how companies listen to their consumers these days. After over twenty years with the same blue-box logo, Gap unveiled a new corporate word-mark on their website on October 4, 2010. Seems harmless enough, right? Redesigning the corporate logo is a rite of passage for new CMOs and new agencies. It happens every day. Company spokesperson Louise Callagy was quoted as saying that the new logo was supposed to mark Gap's transition from "classic, American design to modern, sexy, cool."

But Gap's customers disagreed. Almost immediately, parody logos spelling "Crap" instead of "Gap" were posted, printed on T-shirts and available for sale on the Internet. A parody Twitter account, @GapLogo, began tweeting with attitude. Another parody account, @OldGapLogo, followed. The next day, on YourLogoMakesMeBarf.com, the logo was reviewed. Barbarian Group rode the wave and built a "Crap Logo Yourself" tool that allowed anyone to generate a logo similar to Gap's for their own company. And individual consumers began to design their own Gap logos. Some were ridiculous, some were funny and many were serious works of art.

Within three days of launching their logo, Gap's North American president, Marka Hansen, wrote an open letter in the *Huffington Post*: "From this online dialogue, it's clear that Gap still has a close connection to our customers, so tapping into this energy is right. We've posted a message on the Gap Facebook Page that says we plan to ask people to share their designs with us as well. We welcome the participation we've seen so far."

On October 11, exactly one week after the initial logo was launched, Gap bowed to the reaction of their customers and cancelled all redesigns, returning to their original logo. Marka Hansen explained through an email statement: "There may be a time to evolve our logo, but if and when that time comes, we'll handle it in a different way."

It would have been hard for the Gap executives not to have gotten wind of the social media backlash to their new logo. But much of the social media response to products and services is quieter and is missed by the corporate world. Even for those paying attention, the potential usefulness of the media could be much greater.

When people really listen to what is being said about their company on social media, they get to eavesdrop on a natural and unbiased dialogue about themselves, their company or their competition. They hear concerns, problems, delights, surprises, victories and challenges.

Of course you don't have to stop at your own social media accounts. There are more than enough tools to help you listen. To get instant feedback on our Art Of events, we just follow our hashtag, #TheArtOf. It's a wonderful way to see, in real time, how our audience is reacting to the ideas they are hearing and the way those ideas are delivered. Simple tools like Twitter Search and Google Alerts can be complemented by more elaborate software like Sysomos by Marketwired and Salesforce Marketing Cloud. And there are all sorts of other free and "freemium" options in between. Indeed, there's nothing standing between you and having your ear to the ground in every region of the world.

As columnist Doug Larson has said, "Wisdom is the reward you get for a lifetime of listening when you'd have preferred to talk."

Stopping, looking and listening can help businesses in other ways. Howard Schultz, the former CEO of Starbucks, tells a story about how the powers of observation helped him solve a huge problem at the coffee store chain: weak sales and a dropping stock price. Schultz had just given up his corporate presidency. Without the daily responsibilities of the CEO position, he was able to stop and take a moment to really look at what was going on in the coffee stores. In his words, he "felt like an outsider looking in." He knew that same-store traffic had decreased, and more importantly, the intangible characteristics of the Starbucks experience had been diluted. He just wasn't sure why.

In recent years, in their attempts to gain market share and expand non-coffee revenue, Starbucks had introduced hot sandwiches. Seemed like a good call around the boardroom table. It wasn't until Schultz went back into Starbucks stores—not the office, the stores—that he saw (and smelled) the problem. In his book, *Onward: How Starbucks Fought for Its Life Without Losing Its Soul*, he writes: "Our breakfast sandwiches were selling extremely well, but there was an aroma in the stores that I felt was diluting the integrity of the coffee romance." That aroma was burnt cheese. It was not only overwhelming the glorious smell of coffee, it was also overwhelming the experience. Starbucks was losing the magic that had defined it. In an interview in Toronto, he declared, "We're not in the burnt cheese business" (which, of course, begs the question, "Who is?"). The problem had to be solved, but had he not spent time in the stores wearing his outsider hat, he might not have even found it. Luckily he did.

"By moving the cheese to the top of the sandwich and lowering the baking temperature to about 300°F, the cheese was less likely to burn. The result was, I had to admit, a breakfast offering that was worthy of our coffee."

But as artists show us, stopping, looking and listening can also be the source of creative ideas and innovation. The story of the development of Velcro has been told many times, but it's worth repeating because it's another great example of finding creative inspiration by paying attention to the world around you. Swiss electrical engineer George de Mestral was hunting with his dogs in the Alps. During the outing, he kept having to pick burdock burrs from his pants and the dogs' fur. He noticed how strongly the little seeds adhered to the soft fabric and fluffy fur. That got him wondering about how something so tiny could have such strength and if he might be able to figure out a way to duplicate this amazing property. He brought a few burrs home with him and examined them even more closely under the microscope. That's when he saw the little hooks on the surface of each seed. Then he went about figuring out how to make a material that would feature "hooks" on one side and loops that might be caught by the hooks on the other.

But perhaps our favourite story about the power of "stop, look and listen" comes from a young entrepreneur named Dave Cascino, whom we introduced in Chapter 2.

After dropping out of college, Cascino had travelled across the United States, working various jobs, including at a factory, a tree farm and an Alaska salmon-fishing operation. Eventually he went back to school and landed a job at a trading firm. While there, he learned how to code, and discovered he was pretty good at it. So good, in fact, that he and a friend wrote an algorithm that they were able to sell. Shortly after that, he entered a contest called StartupBus, in which participants work on their own ideas for a start-up company while travelling together on a bus from Silicon Valley to Austin, Texas. The proposals are presented and judged at the SXSW festival. The experience was so fun and exhilarating that when he got home, he decided to continue to pursue ideas for innovative products and companies.

One of these ideas came to him a couple of years later while he walking through Zuccotti Park in New York City. The park was the scene of an Occupy Wall Street protest. Cascino stopped and watched the crowd. What fascinated him was how the protesters were using a "human microphone" to broadcast speeches to the vast sprawl of people. A speaker, without a bullhorn or electronic amplification, would shout out a phrase or sentence and then pause. Next, all those in earshot would, in unison, loudly repeat the words so that those further back could hear them. Once that sentence had been spread through the crowd, the speaker would say her next sentence. It was simple yet powerful. Dave wondered if you could do something like that on the Internet. He went home and immediately started working on a digital version of the human microphone.

That's how he came to develop Thunderclap, a crowd-speaking platform. It allows users to build social media campaigns by collecting Facebook and Twitter posts about issues that users want to draw attention to. Once five hundred supporters have been collected for a given campaign, Thunderclap sends out a message to all of the supporters' followers. Three years later, Thunderclap has over 2.5 million users and is so successful at creating buzz that it has been used by everyone from individual activists to the White House and the United Nations to get important messages out.

Dave Cascino stopped, looked and *listened*. And in doing so, he created something new.

There's no doubt about it—stopping, looking and listening is the key to creative thinking, whether it's in the making of art, the work of innovation or just plain problem solving. Artists let their environment speak to them.

And when it's not talking, they start asking questions.

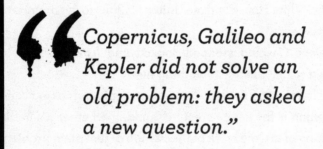

Copernicus, Galileo and Kepler did not solve an old problem: they asked a new question."

—Ken Robinson, educator

ASK QUESTIONS

As anyone who has spent a twelve-hour day with a three-year-old can tell you, kids are not only creative, but intensely curious as well. Small children's seemingly unbroken stream of "Why? Why? Why?" is not only their way of reducing their parents to quivering lumps of exhaustion who will happily give them as many Fruit Roll-Ups as they want in exchange for silence. It's also their way of finding out about the world. But children don't just ask questions of the tired grown-ups around them. They also pose lots of questions to themselves. "What does this crayon taste like?" "Can I ride the dog like a pony?" "What happens if I pour water in Daddy's shoes?" Unfortunately for us and our pets, usually they answer these questions themselves.

Often parents and teachers work overtime to respond to questions before they occur to the little minds. ("This is why we never cut our own hair.") So by the time adulthood is firmly upon us, many of us are out of the habit of asking questions. Or at least we don't ask the kind of questions that we have to answer ourselves. But this is a great pity. Asking questions is one of the best ways to expand our imaginations, to think more originally, to be creative and innovative. And it's something artists never stop doing.

Ask artists about how they do what they do, and time and time again, you'll hear about questions. Many will tell you that they engage in artistic endeavours as a way to explore the questions that occur to them. Dancer, choreographer and artistic director Jasmin Vardimon has said that she gets her inspiration from "questions I can't answer easily." And Joan Didion has explained why she writes: "I write entirely to find out what I'm thinking, what I'm looking at, what I see and what it means. What I want and what I fear. Why did the oil refineries around Carquinez Straits seem sinister to me in the summer of 1956? Why have the night lights in the Bevatron burned in my mind for twenty years? What is going on in these pictures in my mind?"

Tracy Chevalier's novel *Girl with a Pearl Earring* set out to answer the question, *Who exactly is that girl in Vermeer's famous painting?* The film *Memento* seems to be a response to the question, *How could you solve a murder if you had no short-term memory?* And unfortunately for moviegoers everywhere, *Terminator III* addressed the question, *How many limp sequels can you churn out before a story has all of the life choked out of it?*

Some questions are the genesis of a piece of art. Others drive how the art is executed. Author Toni Morrison knew she wanted to write a novel based on the true story of escaped slave Margaret Garner. When Margaret and her children were eventually caught, Margaret killed her own infant daughter to prevent the child suffering a life of slavery. But a question plagued Morrison: Was what Margaret did defensible? About trying to decide how to portray Sethe (the character based on Margaret) and her actions, Morrison has said, "I got to the point where in asking myself who could judge Sethe adequately, since I couldn't, and nobody else that knew her could, really, I felt the only person who could judge her would be the daughter she killed. And from there Beloved inserted herself into the text" (interview with Marsha Darling, 1988).

In a world that reveres experts and loves what is "knowable," the idea of struggling with questions and embracing the fact that you don't know the answers can be as tough as admitting you watch *Hoarders* on TV. But as director Ian Rickson says, "Questions often open the doors of the imagination, even if we feel we should provide answers."

Art is always exploration of a kind. And exploration is driven by questions. So how does the creative thinking that grows out of questions operate once we move outside of the art world? We only have to take a quick look at scientists to find out. In providing us with innovations, discoveries and breakthroughs in understanding, scientists have to be, at their core, creative thinkers. Einstein insisted that scientists were artists, that the only difference between the work the two groups did was in how they expressed their ideas: "If what is seen and experienced is portrayed in the language of logic, then it is science. If it is communicated through forms whose constructions are not accessible to the conscious mind but are recognized intuitively, then it is art." That idea may have your brain stretching in new directions, but who's going argue with Einstein?

Einstein's description of what scientists need to do to be successful also echoes the artists' practice of posing questions to themselves. In *The Evolution of Physics*, which he co-authored with Leopold Infeld, he wrote "The formulation of a problem is often more essential than its solution, which may be merely a matter of mathematical or experimental skill. To raise new questions, new possibilities, to regard old problems from a new angle, requires creative imagination and marks real advance in science."

John Maeda, former professor at the MIT Media Lab and president of the Rhode Island School of Design (RISD), writing a guest blog in *Scientific American*, describes the commonalities between artists and scientists this way:

For those of us involved in either field today (and many of us have a hand in both), we know that the similarities between how artists and scientists work

*far outweigh their stereotypical differences. Both
are dedicated to asking the big questions placed
before us: "What is true? Why does it matter? How
can we move society forward?" Both search deeply,
and often wanderingly, for these answers. We know
that the scientist's laboratory and the artist's
studio are two of the last places reserved for open-
ended inquiry, for failure to be a welcome part of
the process, for learning to occur by a continuous
feedback loop between thinking and doing.*

Maeda reminds us that art and science were not always considered polar opposites but "co-existed naturally." While the scientific world has changed significantly since the time of the great engineer and artist Leonardo da Vinci, Maeda argues that artists can still aid in helping scientists communicate their ideas and navigate the "scientific unknown." The Rhode Island School of Design is spearheading an effort to add art and design to the STEM curriculum in U.S. schools (turning it from STEM to STEAM). And the design school is already helping scientists in their work, says Maeda:

*Artists and designers reformulate the questions
that can guide a project, rethinking or redesigning systems at their base. In this vein, RISD is
collaborating with the University of Rhode Island*

and Brown University on new ways to visualize oceanic data to see the impact of climate change on marine life. The work began with a joint course entitled "The Hypothesis Studio," focusing on the very questions at hand....

Artists and scientists tend to approach problems with a similar open-mindedness and inquisitiveness—they both do not fear the unknown, preferring leaps to incremental steps. They make natural partners.

The business world has certainly begun to realize the importance of asking good questions (not just the "where's that report?" sort). Scroll through any business journal or recent book on leadership, and you are likely to come across articles about the importance of asking the right kinds of questions. In their article, "Relearning the Art of Asking Questions," in the *Harvard Business Review*, Tom Pohlmann and Neethi Mary Thomas explain why people don't ask enough questions, or why the questions they do ask are not truly effective:

Because expectations for decision-making have gone from "get it done soon" to "get it done now" to "it should have been done yesterday," we tend to jump to conclusions instead of asking more questions. And the unfortunate side effect of not asking enough questions is poor decision-making.

That's why it's imperative that we slow down and
take the time to ask more—and better—questions.
At best, we'll arrive at better conclusions. At worst,
we'll avoid a lot of rework later on.

They outline four different types of questions—clarifying, adjoining, elevating and funnelling—that can each lead to different outcomes and encourage truly productive conversations.

In "Become a Company that Questions Everything," in the *Harvard Business Review*, Warren Berger, author of *A More Beautiful Question: The Power of Inquiry to Spark Breakthrough Ideas*, agrees that corporate culture often discourages the "why do we do things this way?" questions that might lead to real changes and improvements, but instead are often seen as disrespectful or just plain inefficient. The powers that be don't want to mess around thinking about how and why things are done. They just want to do more of those same things. But Berger goes on to argue that this attitude is wrong-headed:

For companies seeking to innovate, adapt to
change, and maintain an edge in fast-moving,
competitive markets, a questioning culture can
help ensure that creativity and adaptive think-
ing flows throughout the organization. "One
of the ways successful companies consistently
create separation from the competitive pack is by

critically examining and improving the business model from end to end," says Chris Shimojima, the CEO of Provide Commerce. "This requires a leadership team and work force that is always trying to ask the questions that can light up the big honking issues."

Berger encourages leaders to create environments of inquiry by asking probing, open-ended questions themselves and soliciting the same from their employees. (Google has TGIF question forums during which questions are submitted by everyone in the company and voted on. The most popular questions are put to the big cheeses.) Resources and rewards for question-askers help build the culture, as does avoiding that kryptonite to thoughtful inquiry: "You found the problem, so it's your job to solve it."

The key is that idea of "open-ended" questions—the big whys or what ifs. In essence, these are the kinds of questions that artists and scientists pose themselves and that drive them to create in order to the find the answers. They are the questions of true inquiry and curiosity. And yet, so often, even when we are trying to be creative in our thinking or problem solving, we are hemmed in by asking questions that are simply too prescriptive. And more than likely, we are asking these questions of ourselves because they have been given to us by others. We are being problem solvers instead of problem finders.

Matthew B. Crawford, a professor, philosopher (he has a

Ph.D. in political philosophy from the University of Chicago) and motorcycle mechanic, argues that being problem solvers instead of problem finders means that we focus on entirely the wrong things and our ability to find meaningful answers is impaired. In his bestselling book *Shop Class as Soulcraft* he writes:

> *When you do the math problems at the back of a chapter in an algebra textbook, you are problem solving. If the chapter is entitled "Systems of two equations with two unknowns," you know exactly which methods to use. In such a constrained situation, the pertinent context in which to view the problem has already been determined, so there is no effort of interpretation required. But in the real world, problems don't present themselves in this predigested way; usually there is too much information, and it is difficult to know what is pertinent and what isn't. Knowing what kind of problem you have on hand means knowing what features of the situation can be ignored.*

Daniel Pink, in his book *To Sell Is Human: The Surprising Truth about Moving Others*, argues that problem finders are the people who make the big breakthroughs: "There has been a move from problem solving to problem finding, from solving existing problems to identifying problems people don't realize they have."

The important part of being a problem solver is posing, to yourself and others, all sorts of probing questions. Those in sales might ask about the challenges their customers have or where they are falling short of their objectives. They might ask themselves how their company might help.

Amanda Lang's highly interesting book *The Power of Why* tells stories about how businesses as diverse as shrimp farming and Canadian Tire have created products, revitalized their businesses and made breakthroughs by asking those kinds of open-ended questions. Questions that were not leading and did not focus too narrowly. Questions that indulged in curiosity. Questions that encouraged creative thinking and creative problem solving.

At the heart of all of these open-ended questions is the ability to admit "I don't know." People say that "I'm sorry" are the hardest words to utter. But we would disagree. In a world that has embraced "fake it till you make it," admitting that we don't have the answers can be more than a little tough. Yet as Biz Stone, co-founder of Twitter, acknowledges, "I don't know" gets you much further when you are trying to make improvements. And it was the basis of the approach that he and his team at Twitter agreed to take. "Let's watch and let it be what it needs to be. Let's just agree that we don't know everything, that we don't have all the answers. We don't know very much and other people know more stuff than we do, so why don't we just lean back and watch and then make decisions. It boils down to listening to your customers."

But we've already read about another business person doing just this. When former Starbucks CEO Howard Schultz was faced with dropping revenues, he didn't ask, "How do I raise stock prices?" If he had, he might have started to look at cutting costs or closing locations. Nor did he ask, "How do I get more people into the stores?" Faced with that question, he might simply have launched a new marketing campaign or come up with some short-term promotion, which wouldn't have solved any of his long-term problems. Instead, he asked why. Why weren't some people coming back to Starbucks? Why were they presumably heading to other spots to get their caffeine fix? Asking those kinds of probing, open-ended questions prevented him from going to the pat answers or coming up with standard business quick fixes. They drove him to visit the stores themselves, to "stop, look and listen," and led him to real solutions.

In "How to Accelerate Innovation," (an excerpt from his 2011 book *StandOut*, reprinted in *The Art of Magazine*), Marcus Buckingham provides another great example of the power of questions as part of the creative process. He describes the work of a software engineer this way:

> *[Luke] takes one person's failed coding experiment, reconstructs what the person was trying to do, combines the code with another person's experiment, and creates something neither had initially intended. His genius—although he'd be*

uncomfortable with that label—is asking probing questions without making the original designer defensive, a practice he calls "the Guessing Game."

During his company's once a month code-athons—in which all engineers who want to can stay up the entire night coding, drink a beer or two, munch pizza, and then ship code the next morning—he can be found moving from one engineer to another, playfully guessing where they were intending to take the code, and throwing in a couple of intriguing "guesses" of his own. These guesses, in turn, prompt new ideas from the original designers, which Luke then pieces together into a workable program.

Part of creative exploration is asking "why" questions, but it is also asking the "why not" questions. The story of Toronto's Dufferin Mall is an extraordinary illustration of the power of posing both of these questions when you're looking for creative solutions to difficult problems.

In the early 1990s this west-end shopping centre was a sad, sad place to be on a Saturday afternoon. Serving a neighbourhood that was predominantly low income, the mall was around the corner from busy Bloor Street, bordered by a number of schools and across from a quiet park. As far as location, it was a little hidden. And then there were the shops. Or the lack of them. The mall's anchor store, Eaton's, was a small, anemic branch of the then-still-profitable department store chain. Half of the storefronts were empty; the other retailers evoked the desperate air of a perpetual "going out of business" sale. The food court was dingy and in bad repair, its only patrons the noisy teenagers who spent their lunch hours and skipped classes there. Indeed, troubled teenagers seem to hold the reins at Dufferin Mall. Shoplifting and break-ins were rampant. Gang-related violence erupted on more than one occasion. And then there was a murder in the mall's underground parking garage. If the mall had been noticeably bereft of shoppers before, after the killing, consumers were, as they say, staying away in droves. No doubt about it, Dufferin Mall had all the vibrancy and cheerfulness of a palliative care ward. Or a juvenile detention centre.

Dufferin Mall needed help. And in a big way. So it was a little surprising that its corporate owner brought in David Hall, a manager who had never really dealt with a retail property. But Hall's lack of experience meant that he didn't immediately turn to established retail paradigms—which would probably have meant simply beefing up security, turning the mall into a "fortress," as Hall saw it. Instead he looked at the space and asked, "What's really going on here?"

The mall was in a crowded neighbourhood with plenty of families and seniors—people for whom the ability to do a lot of their shopping under one roof should have been a draw. But then there were all of those teenagers who just wanted a place to go. The mall was clearly filling this need. But what it had to offer—fast food, unsupervised space and small items easily pocketed—was not conducive to the best behaviour. So why not find a way to make their presence productive and to give them a sense of ownership of the space? Why not serve that population in a way that was meaningful to them? Rather than keeping them out, why not draw them in—in a positive way?

Hall approached a local city-run community centre, and the two organizations established Dufferin Mall Youth Services in one of the empty storefronts. They hired a youth worker, whose job it was to both educate the retail employees about youth culture and to provide guidance, counselling and support for the teenagers. The youth worker arranged after-school and summer activities for the kids, including a theatre program and a basketball club that played on an unused portion of the parking lot. But Hall took it one step further. He encouraged a youth employment centre to set up shop in the mall, and then worked with the centre, the local high school and the merchants to create a marketing co-op course at the school. Students would be given short-term jobs with Dufferin Mall merchants, who would also provide lessons and seminars to the co-op cohort. After completing work terms and courses, the students would earn a high-school certificate in retail marketing. The program was a hit, and with their fellow students now part of the mall establishment, the shoplifters and other troublemakers curbed their impulses. In fact, the crime in the mall area dropped by 38 per cent.

Hall also turned his mind to the families in the area. Other than the teens, what was keeping them away? What were their biggest challenges? Hall wondered if shopping with small children didn't make it hard for some parents to spend as much time in the mall as they would like. What about opening a little daycare centre? He certainly had the space. Now let's be honest, managers of struggling retail outlets are not in the habit of giving up potential rent and spending their own money to provide free services. But why not? Hall spruced up one of the empty retail spaces, filled it with extruded plastic and hired some qualified caregivers. In no time, the room was bursting with delighted kids whose parents were hitting the stores unencumbered by restless offspring.

And what about the seniors? They may not have had the consumer needs of the families, but malls are usually popular places for seniors to get inexpensive lunches or some sheltered walking. How could he encourage the seniors to come back to the mall? Hall decided to focus on the food court. He improved the lighting, added skylights and got rid of all the existing tables and chairs. He then installed tables and chairs that were bolted to the floor in configurations that sat only two or four people. Now the seniors didn't have to navigate around huge noisy clusters of teenagers if they wanted a seat. And with more families and seniors taking up space in the food court, it was a far less attractive place for the kids to spend their days.

Eventually Hall invited a community newspaper and a literacy program to share some of the mall's ample floor space. He worked with the city and community groups to improve facilities and programs at the park across the street and throughout the neighbourhood. The mall manager had even more ambitious plans, including a land swap with the high school so the mall could face busy Bloor Street and the schools could face the park, but the hard economic times of the early 1990s scuttled that agreement. Still, the customers returned and, with the renewed traffic, the mall was able to attract more and more retailers, which in turn allowed for additional renovations. (They even managed to poke fun at this transformation with an ad campaign created by our friends at Brees Communications that used the tag line "Dufferin Mall. Really?")

Today, if you visit Dufferin Mall, you are not likely to see Hall's first creative solutions. There is no longer a youth employment centre (although there is a Service Canada office) and you won't find a daycare. That's because the space is crammed with thriving retailers. But it can *still* be a miserable place to spend a Saturday afternoon—if you don't like the press of crowds and a two-hour lap to find a parking spot.

RON TITE'S FIRST JOB out of university is another great tale about the power of asking questions to propel creative thinking.

Ron's degree was in phys. ed., but after graduation he landed a position with Queen's Business School, working as a program manager to help launch its national executive MBA program, the first EMBA in the country to be delivered over video conferencing. The program was being developed under the watchful eye of David Anderson, dean of the School of Business. Gordon Cassidy, a professor of statistics at Queen's, was the visionary director of the program, and Barb Shopland, a Bell executive, was one of the first corporate champions of the initiative. The rest of the team was made up of a small group of young hires—many, like Ron, with little or no experience working in technology or business.

The program they set out to create would involve all sorts of "firsts." The professors hadn't taught over video conferencing before, students hadn't learned through the medium before, and the telecommunication companies hadn't struck a partnership of that magnitude before. No one knew how the exams would work, or how the student groups would do homework in between class sessions. It wasn't at all clear how a class culture would develop.

The program could have been called a start-up, but the high tuition cost and outstanding reputation of the university meant that the program couldn't really be treated as a beta version of the real thing. This was an MBA. From Queen's. With some of the brightest and most successful people in the country enrolled. In order to get the program up and running *well* straight out of the gate, its architects were going to have to address a number of challenges.

Working within an academic environment, with tenured professors chiming in on school matters, is never easy. You think wrangling a bunch of partners in an accounting firm is difficult? Try waltzing into an ivory tower and telling a bunch of silver-haired Ph.D.s that you're going to deliver classes to CEOs over broadband using relatively new video technology—and charge thousands of dollars for it. Birkenstocks flew. The team had to be creative.

Once the university itself was on board, the program managers had to find a way to come up with an affordable telemarketing plan. Calculated at then-current rates, the video-conferencing costs looked like a line item on a NASA budget. The team had to be creative.

The group also had to convince the business school faculty that instead of walking down to the hall to a lecture theatre, the profs would drive to a studio three hours away in Ottawa and teach to a camera with only a technician in the room. Not the liveliest classroom environment—and a pretty long commute by anyone's standards. The team had to be creative.

- They had to be creative in delivery.
- They had to be creative in finance.
- They had to be creative in process.
- They had to be creative in operations.
- They had to be creative in sales.
- They had to be creative in human resources.

The university was, of course, filled with experts in all of those areas. But Gordon Cassidy didn't appeal to any of them for help. Instead, he relied on his group of "non-experts." By the time he launched the second year of the program, he had four program managers working in the national executive MBA, and two in the Ottawa-based executive MBA. Of the six, four were phys. ed. grads, like Ron. Yup, to help deliver the most innovative and cutting edge professional graduate programs at one of the most respected academic institutions in the country, Cassidy turned to four people who had taken ballroom dancing, winter camping and "Games of Lower Organization."

When Ron asked Cassidy why, the director said, "You're all perfect for this environment because you're social, you're competitive and you know how to play and win on a team. I don't need accountants or marketers; I need people who can work together to solve the problems we don't even know we have." What Cassidy was doing was avoiding "experts" who would immediately know and reference what had worked in the past, who would rely on what had been done before to solve the problems *as they perceived them*. What he wanted were fresh thinkers who weren't afraid to challenge the status quo, in part because they didn't know what that was.

The young people on the team were, not surprisingly, full of questions. *Would this work? Could we try this? What if we approached it like that?* They didn't have answers at their fingertips. They had questions.

They put those questions to use in trying to solve the telecommunications cost problem. Very few, if any, businesses and institutions were using the quantity of broadband that an online video-conferencing degree would consume. The telecommunications companies weren't, therefore, ready with bulk rates and high-volume discounts. But even as the group began negotiating for some sort of deal, they wondered if a little bartering might drop the costs further. At whom was this MBA aimed, after all? Executives. What did the telcos have plenty of? Executives. They asked the telcos if they wanted to have some of their emerging leaders join the inaugural cohort—in exchange for reduced telecom fees. The telecommunications companies agreed. It was a brilliant plan. The EMBA would be able to meet its budget, and the companies would be able to experience their technologies being put to new use—and perhaps be inspired to think of other new markets and sales potential.

It was a great solution, but given its "swap meet" approach, not one that was likely to come from an accounting professor.

Queen's EMBA turned out to be a huge success. Of course, it won its reputation because of the quality of the education it provided and the talented and dedicated faculty that gave the courses. But there's no doubt that Gordon Cassidy's understanding of the importance of creative thinking was a huge factor in getting the program off the ground in the first place. By hiring people who were full of questions instead of answers, he created a team that could both identify and solve problems, who could connect the dots in a new way and who could make something different actually work.

The questioning was a huge component in the success of the program launch. But then again, Ron and his team were a group who exhibited another hallmark of the creative folk: *they got things done.*

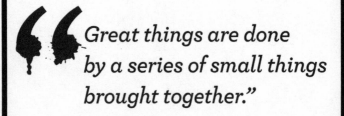 *Great things are done by a series of small things brought together."*

—Vincent van Gogh

GET 'ER DONE

You may not be a big fan of the comedy of Larry the Cable Guy, but you have to admit, he's got a snappy catch phrase. Larry, with his plaid shirt and baseball cap, polishes off his rough-hewn observations with the rallying cry "Get 'er done." It's Larry's version of "Just do it!"—an exhortation to stop with the excuses, to quit messing around, to start doing what you need to be doing.

Thanks to Nike's brilliant marketing campaign, most of us are aware of the need to get off the couch, but what about getting off our intellectual butts? In our intellectual and creative lives, if artists show us one thing, it's the importance of "getting 'er done."

Paul Winston, a physiatrist now in his forties, is on his second career. His first was as a professional dancer with

Canada's National Ballet. After six years of dancing with the company, a bicycle accident and shoulder injury made Winston think about other careers. At the age of twenty-six he left the ballet and went to university and later to med school. But he didn't leave everything about his dance training behind. Just like Dr. John Semple, whom we met in the Introduction, Winston applies observational skills he learned in his art in his work as a doctor. Specializing in rehabilitation medicine, Winston likes to spend considerable amounts of time watching his patients move, rather than relying on the questioning techniques most of his fellow practitioners use to find the source of their patients' problems. But the other part of his dance background that has been invaluable in his new career is the ability to work hard. Really hard.

In her August 2015 *Globe and Mail* profile of Winston, Marsha Lederman writes about how dance helped Winston with the demands of med school: "The discipline he learned at the ballet had him wondering about fellow students who came to class unprepared—having not done the reading, for example. 'People wouldn't put up their hands, they wouldn't speak. The fact that they had no interest, I found that really [shocking] because I was trained to work hard all the time. I couldn't not work hard,' he explains. . . . 'The sheer brute force work is easy for me because of the dance background.'"

Anyone who has seen photographs of dancers' gnarled feet will not be surprised to hear that dancers must work hard to execute their art. Dance is, after all, both an art and a demanding physical act. But dance is certainly not the only art that relies on hard work. In fact, *all* art does.

Hard work is not, however, something we always think of when we think of art. It would be an interesting experiment to do a little informal poll on the street in which you asked various passersby to describe "an artist's lifestyle." It would be even more interesting if you broke it down by the type of artist. For a rock and roll songwriter and musician you might hear about booze and drug-filled parties packed with groupies. For a painter or a sculptor, people might describe hanging out in airy loft studios or galleries or sitting in front of a canvas along the River Seine. A poet might be imagined in a cramped, dark underground club, reading a poem or two before joining his hip fellow poets for a drink. An actor might be jet-setting around the world before collapsing on a chaise longue beside a Malibu pool. We suspect that what you wouldn't hear would be, "Up at six thirty, seven latest. At the easel by eight. Paint until five. Have a bite to eat. Back to the easel. Clean up at ten and then to bed." And yet for most people working as professional artists, that's probably closer to their reality.

(Okay, there may be a tiny grain of truth in some of the stereotypes about artists. David Bowie claimed that he remembered absolutely nothing about making his album *Station to Station*. He did, however, remember doing a lot of cocaine. But most artists work enormously hard at what they do. And while Bowie no doubt did a little partying in his *Station to Station* days, the "drugs" part of rock and roll appeared to help him work—as well as play.)

Arts journalist Sarah Thornton explains that while we sometimes don't realize the sheer quantity of effort that it takes to make art, it's what leads to great artistic achievements: "Being a full-time artist—rather than a weekend hobbyist—takes a great deal of discipline. It is hard work even when it looks like play. Artists sometimes cover up their industriousness by posing as self-indulgent wastrels but, in my experience, artists with high recognition are the kind of workaholics who revolve their holidays around work and have no plan to retire."

In a *Huffington Post* interview, Clara Lieu, a visual artist and professor at the Rhode Island School of Design, talks about a number of students she either went to school with or taught who, despite their talent, didn't become professional artists or see any growth in their work, simply because they didn't push themselves or put in the elbow grease. As she explains, talent is only one part of what makes someone an artist: "All the talent in the world won't get you anywhere if you aren't willing to work hard, push your boundaries, and try new approaches."

But if you want to hear about the importance of actually sitting down and getting 'er done, just listen to the artists themselves.

Painter and photographer Chuck Close is blunt: "Inspiration is for amateurs. The rest of us just show up and get to work." Eighteenth-century British painter Sir Joshua

Reynolds was a bit more verbose when addressing his Royal Academy students:

> *You must have no dependence on your genius. If you have great talents, industry will improve them; if you have but moderate abilities, industry will supply their deficiency. Nothing is denied to well directed labour; nothing is to be obtained without it. Not to enter into metaphysical discussions on the nature or essence of genius, I will venture to assert, that assiduity unabated by difficulty, and a disposition eagerly directed to the object of its pursuit, will produce effects similar to those which some call the result of natural powers.*

American composer John Adams puts it this way: "My experience has been that most really serious creative people I know have very, very routine and not particularly glamorous work habits. Because creativity, particularly the kind of work I do—which is writing large-scale pieces, either symphonic music or opera music—it's just, it's very labour intensive."

Many, many artists talk about the importance of routine in getting their work done (writers David Foster Wallace and Marilynne Robinson are notable exceptions), but it doesn't always come easily. Playwright Tom Stoppard, in fact, had such a tough time sitting down to work (he described this as his "ineffectual inefficiency") that at one point, he even chained himself to his desk to force himself to write. It didn't work. But even Stoppard's desperate self-shackling is testimony to the fact that he recognized that you really have to work to create anything.

Of course, it makes sense that being an artist involves *doing*. But *all* creativity is a process, is about producing. We can't really say that we are working creatively if we only sit around sipping lattes and thinking about new ways of doing things but never trying them. Committing that sentence to paper, however, reminds us of one of the great scenes in Woody Allen's classic movie *Annie Hall*. Two "creative" types are talking at a Hollywood party and one is saying, "Right now, it's only a notion. But I think I can get money to make it into a concept. And later turn it into an idea." It's one of the many things about LA that makes Woody's character Alvy Singer so nauseated that he can't make it to his TV interview.

Despite what may or may not happen in La-La Land, no matter how creative our solutions might be to whatever problems we face, if we don't act, we won't get anywhere.

Ken Robinson puts it this way: "Being creative involves *doing* something. It would be odd to describe someone who never did anything as creative. To call somebody creative suggests they are actively producing something in a deliberate way. People are not creative in the abstract; they are creative *in* something: in mathematics, in engineering, in writing, in music, in business, in whatever. Creativity involves putting your imagination to work. In a sense, creativity is applied imagination."

In his award-winning and thought-provoking book *Outliers: The Story of Success*, Malcolm Gladwell drew wide public attention to a study done by K. A. Ericsson and A. C. Lehmann. The two researchers looked at athletes, among other groups, to determine the common factor in the lives and habits of highly successful people. What they discovered was that all of those who were making extraordinary achievements had one thing in common: at least ten thousand hours working at their particular skill.

That number of hours sounds daunting at first. After all, working forty hours a week, it would take five years to rack up ten thousand hours. What's more, the idea that we need to put in thousands of hours before we become truly proficient at something seems to ring false when we hear stories about twenty-something investment wizards or teenaged technology wunderkinds. These young men and women, barely off their acne medication but setting the Dow and the Nasdaq ablaze with innovative video games, apps, and all sorts of new technology, appear to be geniuses. How else to explain the phenomenal break-throughs they are achieving while some of us more seasoned folks are still trying to figure out how to create a "genius" list on our iPods?

What we sometimes fail to recognize is that these young innovators, brilliant as they no doubt are, and fuelled by intense passion for what they do, put in many more hours on their work than we might imagine. Gladwell points out that people like Bill Gates and Bill Joy (creator of the UNIX software system and writer of much of the code for Java) made innovative breakthroughs in software development while they still had all their hair, because, through a series of often lucky breaks, they were able to spend enormous amounts of time on computers in an era, unlike the present one, when unlimited access was very rare indeed.

A more recent example is young Palmer Luckey, inventor of the wonderfully named virtual reality headset Oculus Rift. Luckey was born in Long Beach, California, in 1992, and was home-schooled before starting community college courses at fourteen. Allowed to explore his own interests from a very young age (and with the time to do so), Luckey became fascinated with all sorts of electronics. By his early teens he was tinkering with Tesla coils, electromagnetic coil guns and lasers. He was also modifying various types of computer hardware, including gaming consoles, and teaching himself engineering along the way. But his most intense fascination was with virtual reality technology. He began fixing iPhones, doing boat repair and working as a sailing instructor in order to earn money to buy virtual reality headsets—amassing a collection of over fifty different models in a few years. But he wasn't satisfied by any of the technology available. Even the VR gear designed for the military was clunky and provided not so much a "virtual reality" experience as a rather wonky reality approximation that often induced car-sickness in its users. So he started designing his own VR headsets. He finished his first prototype labouring in his parents' garage. He was just eighteen.

Luckey then posted about his VR headset on a number of online forums. One of those descriptions caught the eye of John Carmack, an influential video game developer. Carmack asked to see Luckey's prototype and was wowed by what he found. The device represented a huge step forward in resolution, field of view, weight and affordability. Carmack made some modifications and wrote some custom code so that some of the big games his company produced could support VR headsets. This ignited a wave of interest in virtual reality gaming. The enthusiasm for the headsets was so intense that Carmack left his company, Luckey dropped out of university, and together with several other enthusiastic financial backers and funds raised through a Kickstarter campaign, they set out to form their own company and develop the Oculus Rift for retail sales. The Oculus Rift has been described as "revolutionary." According to *Fortune* magazine, Facebook founder Mark Zuckerberg has called it "one of the coolest things" he's ever seen. (He ended up buying the company for $2 billion.)

No doubt about it, Palmer Luckey has achieved remarkable things for someone so very young. His innovation was quickly embraced by the likes of HTC (a smartphone manufacturer) and Steam (one of the largest gaming companies in the world), who have teamed up to create their own headset. Sony has announced a competing headset, and Google launched Google Cardboard in response. (Virtual reality technology is also finding its way into the worlds of architecture, engineering and medicine, among others.)

But it's also interesting to note the timeline here. The home-schooled Luckey had been building and modifying electronics and virtual reality devices for seven years before he created the set that caught Carmack's attention. He had been, in other words, working his creative muscle for thousands and thousands of hours. Sure, Palmer Luckey is a wunderkind. But he's a hardworking one.

While those of us working at The Art Of haven't invented anything as groundbreaking as the Oculus Rift, we long ago discovered the power of getting 'er done. When we begin to plan a new speaking series, we start by discussing the possible theme for the event. (That is the point when we feel as if we are facing a blank canvas.) We bounce around a number of ideas before settling on one. Once we decide on the focus, we brainstorm to identify our expectations. They are often pretty unrealistic. But we don't worry about that. Instead, we spend our time on trying to execute the idea and fulfill those expectations. In other words, we spend less time thinking about painting and more time actually painting. Usually in the end, the energy we put into working on our goals gets us far closer to realizing them than we would have ever thought possible. We are convinced that this approach allows us to be much more creative in our offerings than we might be otherwise.

So hard work is essential to any creative endeavour. But another way the "get 'er done" attitude works to improve creativity and creative thinking is that by putting new ideas into practice, we are often led to other new ideas.

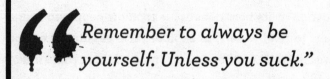

Remember to always be yourself. Unless you suck."

—Joss Whedon, screenwriter/director

In other words, creativity tends to lead to more creativity. Anyone who has checked one small fact on Wikipedia, only to look up from the screen two hours later and realize that they've travelled from the entry on the Magna Carta to an article about Dolly Parton, by way of the page on dysentery and the log on molecular genetics, understands how intellectual curiosity has a habit of growing once we indulge it. Talking with *Forbes* magazine about his book *In Defense of a Liberal Education*, journalist Fareed Zakaria argues that intellectual curiosity is the most valuable part of a liberal education: "What a liberal education at its best does . . . is to allow people to range widely, to read widely, to explore their passions. Let one interest lead to another and on and on. I think that kind of breadth and the ability to feed your curiosity and indulge [it] is incredibly important. It's what, now in the corporate world, one would call synergy, or out-of-the-box thinking, or the intersection of disciplines. This has always been a central part of what a liberal education has meant."

Indeed, given the right environment, ideas tend to multiply.

The Blue Man Group is a great example of this kind of creative reproduction at work. These performance artists now have permanent shows in New York, Boston, Chicago, Orlando and Las Vegas, and a touring company that takes them to forty cities a year in such places as Canada, the U.S., Australia, Germany and Brazil. They've performed all over the world, toured with Moby, were nominated for a Grammy and have made numerous television appearances on shows like *Ellen* and *The Tonight Show*. Inarguably, Blue Man Group is a massive global artistic success (even if Tobias Fünke of *Arrested Development* initially thought it was a support group for sad guys).

Even with all the accolades, it's still hard to fathom how Blue Man Group ever got started. One typically doesn't just wake up one morning and decide to be a speechless PVC percussionist or to sculpt with regurgitated marshmallows (let alone put that skill on stage and charge people to see it).

Here's how it actually got going. Old friends Chris Wink, Matt Goldman and Phil Stanton were roommates living in Manhattan's Lower East Side in 1988. They had an idea. They thought it would be funny to hold a funeral procession in Central Park for the decade that was about to pass away. They would say goodbye to the 1980s by parading through the park as bald—and blue—mourners.

Now most people would stop there. They'd laugh about the idea, but they would never get around to actually doing it. Chris, Matt and Phil, however, did. The three friends put on bald wigs, covered themselves in blue paint and walked through the park carrying a casket filled with symbols of all the things about the decade that they were happy to say adios to, including a Rambo doll and a tiny model of the Berlin Wall.

After the procession, Chris, Matt and Phil started to perform as the Blue Man (an echo of "human") characters on the street. You don't become a street performer because you're in it for the money. You do it because you're in it for the art. As Phil explained: "We wanted to have a connection to our own personal creativity. We weren't necessarily sculptors, or painters. We played some music, but not at the quality to be in a philharmonic, but we all felt creative and a yearning to live a creative lifestyle. The Blue Man character was our vehicle for doing all those things."

What would eventually become the Blue Man theatre performances came from the group's initial creation of that "Blue Man" character. At first they simply walked around the city in their Blue Man getup, gauging the reaction, stopping to chat with the people gaping at them. Then they moved to the small stage in NYC. They played music. They worked on the comedy of their act. Eventually they added lights, electronics, paint and more. They continued to try new things. Ideas fed off of other ideas. Before they knew it, they had a stage show ready for Vegas and many of the other great entertainment centres of the world.

From a corporate perspective, in the early years you could have called Blue Man Group an early-stage start-up with nothing but an interesting idea. Their street performances could be defined as their discovery phase, where they tested the public's reaction to the characters. Still, they didn't exactly go out and pitch venture capitalists. How could they? *Okay, so the show has three characters— all blue. They don't say anything, but that's okay because there really isn't a plot. What we are going to do is play PVC pipes as drums, rhythmically chew Cap'n Crunch cereal, spit paint onto canvases and unfurl rolls of toilet paper into crowds. We might do something with chewed marshmallows. We're still beta-testing that. We figure 200K will get us going. Are you in?*

Building the company, expanding into other cities, hiring and training new cast members, recording their albums, and steadily preparing the entrepreneurial venture for growth wasn't easy. But you can get people to do that kind of work. You can bring in seasoned CEOs, hire accountants, buy software, listen to consultants and more to put in the hours needed. The most difficult step Blue Man took was that first creative one: that small idea about painting themselves blue and walking through the park with a casket. They didn't have fans. They didn't have proof of concept. They didn't have money. They just had an idea and the guts to do it.

Poet and philosopher Lao Tzu famously said, "The journey of a thousand miles begins with a single step." (We don't know who would want to go on a thousand-mile walking journey, but if you do, we'd recommend stretching first.) Despite the proverb's popularity, we've never really liked it. If you want to inspire someone to take a first step, it's probably best not to describe the surely horrible thousand-mile journey that will follow. Perhaps we are just easily daunted by the thought of chafing and sunburn, but if we were going to put a motivational poster on our office wall, it might be "The journey of the first step begins with a single step." After all, in a world that demands creativity, deciding on a final destination may be counterproductive. Instead, we should focus on the "doing," on the process, on the exploration of new terrain.

You need to take the first step and see where you want to plant the next one. It may not lead you on a long journey, but it might. If it does, you can change direction or retrace your steps as you go. Beginning anything new—whether it is starting a family, moving to a new city, embarking on a corporate restructuring or even just changing the way we think—can be hugely intimidating. But walking into Central Park for a parade is just fun. Taking that first step is the important part. It may inspire a second step and a third. But focusing on what you are doing in the moment, instead of worrying about the next step, will keep you going—and may lead to more inspiration. The Blue Man Group didn't plan for success; success just happened organically. It wasn't about the journey. It was about the steps.

Taking steps—even if most of them don't lead anywhere, or you end up in a series of one-step adventures for a while—requires time and effort. We imagine that most of our readers know all about hard work. Raising kids, running your household, doing your job, volunteering in your community—most people are so busy that fifteen minutes in a hot shower seems as idle as a week-long spa getaway.

But here we have to return to the importance of "stopping" that we talked about in Chapter 4. We are reminded that creativity often requires that you remove yourself from the daily treadmill. What are you working really hard *at*? Are you spending the time working on creative thinking or creative endeavours? Are you keeping that muscle toned?

You may indeed have an active creative life—even if your profession doesn't involve a lot of creativity. Perhaps you play in a garage band or write fiction in your spare time. Maybe you focus your creative energies on landscape gardening or on nature photography. Nurturing the creative self has enormous benefits—from relaxation to a broadening of the imagination to feelings of empowerment derived from producing things that please us and are admired by others.

And some creative activities have been shown to have direct links to abilities in other areas. Numerous studies suggest that math and music are closely tied. (Einstein claimed that if he hadn't been a physicist, he would have been a musician. He credited music and his time at the piano with leading him to a great many of his scientific insights, although his descriptions suggest that music may have been an occupation that let his mind wander and unlocked his unconscious creativity.) Reading and writing fiction encourages empathy, compassion and a greater understanding of the human condition.

Creativity is, after all, about making connections that have not been made before, noticing unusual analogies, and seeing what isn't there. If you write poetry, paint watercolours or dance, you are more likely to be able to apply your creativity to other things. But that isn't always a given. Sometimes you have to make a conscious effort to transfer the kind of creative flexibility you are exploring in your community theatre work to other areas where creative thinking would help your life and labour. In order to do that, you have to identify the kind of creativity you need in your life, and then put the work in there. After all, if you aren't working your creative muscle in that area, next time you have to come up with a different way to handle client needs or a creative solution to survive the holidays with your extended family, you are as likely to be successful as Jabba the Hutt doing an Iron Man.

Many people who become adept at creative endeavours or creative approaches to life and business have to first find ways to put in the time. While some of the most "creative" companies now recognize that *they* benefit if employees have "work time" to spend on their own projects, some of this attitude may just be smoke and mirrors. According to Nicholas Carlson, writing in *Business Insider* magazine, Marissa Mayer, CEO of Yahoo and former Google employee, has said that the Google 20% time (devoted to personal projects during the workweek) is a myth. "It's really 120 per cent time," she says. Her point is that Google employees put in so much overtime at their job that even if they are working on a personal project at 10:00 a.m. on a Thursday, they are essentially on their own time.

That may sound discouraging, but it suggests that the innovative types at Google are really working with the same time restraints as Howard at Revenue Canada and

Mary at Vancouver General Hospital. Just like the folks at Google, we need to *make* time to exercise our creative energies.

Markus "Notch" Persson is an interesting example of "finding the time." Markus is one of those guys who seems to have been born with a keyboard under his fingers. When he was seven, his father brought home a computer—a Commodore 128. Fascinated, the young boy started tinkering with it, writing his first program at the age of eight. The following years were tough ones for Persson, but he found solace from his social challenges at school and a difficult family life in the intricate binary world. In his early twenties, he was still living at home, still working on his coding projects in isolation. His mother urged him to take an online computer coding course. The course eventually helped him land a job at the computer game developer Midasplayer (which became King.com, the maker of Candy Crush Saga).

Being a games developer is creative work, so Persson was certainly putting hours into exercising his creative muscle. The problem was that the ideas that really interested him were ones that were outside of the work he was doing for King.com. He and another developer at King, Jakob Porsér, began working on these games in their off hours, much to the chagrin of the execs who weren't keen on Persson and Porsér creating competition for their own products.

Eventually Persson solved his employer's problem by moving to jAlbum, an online photo-sharing site. It was a counterintuitive move. He was no longer working in an industry devoted to his first love, computer gaming. And there's no doubt that spending his days writing code so that people could post their holiday pics didn't stretch his creative muscles the way game design did. But jAlbum didn't care what Persson did in his own time—if he wanted to stay up until two in the morning tinkering with a video game, what did it matter to them? Whatever he created would be of no threat to their business. With this arrangement, Persson was able to devote his game-design energy to his own projects. And one of those after-work projects just happened to be an unremarkable-looking "sandbox" game called Minecraft.

Shortly after appearing in the indie gaming universe, Minecraft took off. Both Porsér and Persson quit their jobs to work on it full time, before eventually selling the game and the company that grew out of it to Microsoft for $2.5 billion. By finding a way to make time to really exploit his creative energies, Persson created the biggest-selling computer game of all time.

Many workplaces do want employees to think more creatively on the clock. At least that's what they tell us at the annual team-building and innovation getaways. But while they may *preach* creative thinking and innovation, few deliver.

Why? It's simple: Organizations don't change, people do. An organization is just the sum of all the efforts of all the people within it—people like you and like us—who make individual decisions every single day. When you combine all the decisions made by all the people, you end up with a company that is innovative or one that is not.

So it's great to preach innovation from the C-suite but until employees feel they have a green light to start making different decisions, to start thinking more creatively and to put this creativity into action, corporate culture—and the work a company or organization does—doesn't budge one bit from its status quo. The powers that be might as well cancel the brainstorming and innovation workshops at the Whistler off-site and just let everyone ski and snow-board. It may be tougher to justify, but just as much will be accomplished.

The point is that, just like artists, organizations and their employees can't truly be creative or innovative unless they actually do the work. They have to put ideas into action, take the first steps and walk the walk. And this can't be a one-off approach. Let's say that you are struggling with a way to combine the demands of your job with your new responsibilities as a volunteer hockey coach. You are likely to be more successful in coming up with creative solutions if you've been working on "thinking outside the box" in other areas of your life and work. But even if you do happen on a great new way of doing things, keep in mind that if you stop challenging yourself, you may not be up to the task the next time you want to be really creative. Creativity is a muscle. It needs to be exercised. Take it from the artists.

There appears to be evidence that young people have an easier time accessing creativity than older folks. At eighty-nine, the Nobel Prize–winning novelist Doris Lessing gave vent to this dour view: "Don't imagine you'll have it forever. Use it while you've got it because it'll go; it's sliding away like water down a plug hole."

But the careers of other artists suggest that it is really a case of "use it or lose it." Fyfe Dangerfield, musician, songwriter and founding member of the indie rock band Guillemots, describes the process this way:

> I used to think that being inspired was about sitting around waiting for ideas to come to you. That can happen occasionally: sometimes, I'm walking down the street and suddenly hear a fragment of music that I can later work into a song. But generally, it's not like that at all. I liken the process to seeing ghosts: the ideas are always there, half-formed. It's about being in the right state of mind to take them and turn them into something that works.
>
> One of the most difficult things about writing music is the sheer number of distractions: mobiles, email, Twitter, YouTube. When you're writing, you have to be very disciplined, to the point of being awkward: turn off your phone and find a space to work without any of these distractions. . . .

*Your creativity is like a tap: if you don't use it,
it gets clogged up.*

Composer George Gershwin would have no doubt agreed with Dangerfield—at least about the importance of exercising your creativity if you want to keep it. "Like the pugilist," Gershwin said, "the songwriter must always keep in training."

The problem with competition is that it takes away the requirement to set your own path, to invent your own method, to find a new way."

—Seth Godin, author

NO COMPETITION

A few years ago, we had the opportunity to watch Art Battle in Toronto. For those who have never been before, let us explain the concept. Remember *American Gladiators*? Well, it's like that but for artists, who apply paint to canvases rather than to their faces. Cheered on by their supporters and accompanied by a DJ, local artists have twenty minutes to paint an original work of art and the audience votes on their favourites. There are two rounds with the top two vote-getters in each round advancing to the finals for painting supremacy. The finished works are sold in a silent auction following the competition. Art Battle runs these events all across the country and even hosts a national championship. It's live competitive painting, and not unlike a sports event—except there's no jockstraps, helmets or overused clichés about giving 110 per cent.

If you are anything like us, the thought of competitive painting brings a smile to your face. And like us, you might be wondering: *Are there referees? Will there be replays of the winning brush strokes aired on a big screen? Do smock-pulling fights ever break out between the painters?*

One of the most entertaining things about Art Battle is that the events seem counter to everything people understand about the process of making art. We think of artists as working in the privacy of their own studios or homes, engaged in a solitary exercise where they can take time to experiment and explore their ideas. And while the rest of us may, in the end, judge the results of the process, during the creative act itself, there are few witnesses. (There aren't many artists who would give out backstage passes to their deepest and most personal exploration.) But during an Art Battle competition, artists put themselves in the middle of an arena armed with only their supplies and a looming clock that counts down the time. And there's the whole idea of art being a "battle." It just sounds wrong.

That being said, we have to admit that it isn't as if conflict and rivalry don't exist in the art world. The world of letters is full of competitive feuds: Fitzgerald and Hemingway, Norman Mailer and Gore Vidal, V. S. Naipaul and Paul Theroux, sisters A. S. Byatt and Margaret Drabble. Author Mary McCarthy got herself sued after she delivered this brutal takedown of Lillian Hellman during an appearance on *The Dick Cavett Show*: "Every word she writes is a lie. Including 'and' and 'the.'"

In the visual arts, nothing quite compares to the contest between the greats Leonardo da Vinci and Michelangelo, who were asked to execute paintings of different battle scenes side by side on the interior walls of the Council House of the Palazzo Vecchio in Florence. Even at the time, it was considered a "contest" and engendered such bitterness between the painters that they hurled insults at each other's work for years after. (Unbelievably, the resulting artwork was painted over about fifty years later during what is surely the most misguided redecorating effort in the whole of human history.) Matisse and Picasso also thought of each other as rivals, and the nineteenth-century painter J. M. W. Turner seemed to consider all master painters, past and present, as his competition.

In the world of music, you might think of the Rolling Stones and the Beatles (although it was apparently more of a contest between their managers than the musicians themselves). There are, however, a number of musicians who have gotten into dust-ups with each other, whether it's about cultural appropriation (Iggy Azalea and Azealia Banks), generational conflict (Wynton Marsalis and Miles Davis), or formal recognition (for the love of God, Kanye, just give one of your own Grammys to Beyoncé and let it rest.) And sadly, some of these musical rivalries have been deadly: the tensions between East and West Coast rappers cost Tupac and The Notorious B.I.G. their lives.

With all of these contests, there's plenty of emotion to be sure, but scratch below the surface and you'll quickly see that the competition is almost always "after the fact." It takes place outside of the creative endeavour, once the work is out in the world, meeting its fate. There are exceptions. J. M. W. Turner, exhibiting at the same 1832 Royal Academy show as John Constable, waited until Constable had left the building. Turner inspected Constable's work, *The Opening of Waterloo Bridge*, then returned to his own seascape painting, pulled out his paints and added a splash of red to the centre. Turner's canvas ended up overshadowing Constable's work at the show.

But the Turner story is unusual because most artists are not thinking about others in the actual moments when they are engaged in their own art. In fact, most people involved in creative endeavours note that the periods of the most productivity are marked by a complete and utter absorption with the task—a focus so strong that the passage of time, physical discomforts (like hunger) and even the artists' own emotions simply aren't on the radar. Artist Keith Haring puts it this way: "When it is working, you completely go into another place, you're tapping into things that are totally universal, completely beyond your ego and your own self. That's what it's all about."

(This kind of mental transport has been recognized for centuries—and it occurs with activities other than making art or being engaged in creative endeavours. It's sometimes referred to as "flow" or, more recently, as "being in the zone.")

But this isn't the only reason most artists reject the idea of competition. Before the Art Battle we watched, we had the opportunity to chat with some of the artists. We acknowledged that the Art Battle was an artificial kind of event, but we wondered about whether or not they felt that other artists were their direct competitors at other times. After all, the general public has a limited attention span when it comes to any sort of entertainment, and finite dollars to spend on supporting the arts and acquiring artworks. Despite that reality, most of the artists we talked to said that there was no such thing as competition in the art world. They felt that if artists are unique and their expression is true to their vision and their values, there's no one else who can do what they do. They aren't competing against anyone else because no one is shaped by the same personal experiences that inform and inspire their work. Others may do the same thing but they can't possibly *create* the same thing.

So we come back to our original discussion of what we mean when we call someone an "artist." Part of that definition is that the artist's work is original and authentic. Certainly, authenticity means being true to yourself—expressing your own ideas and beliefs in a way that is meaningful for you. But the truth is, there aren't many artists who can say that they are unequivocally free to pursue their passion without any intervention from the customers who buy the work or the institutions that provide financial support.

Just when they think they're free to pursue their art, the network sends over some notes from the broadcast standards people, the gallery owner calls and says she can't accommodate the request for the smoke machine, the jazz club emails that their drums won't fit on stage, the festival calls and says the last dance number will have to be twenty seconds shorter, or the organizer of the poetry slam contest asks them to kindly remember who the sponsors are.

It's kind of like your last job. Remember when your boss told you that he wasn't a micromanager and preferred to completely empower his team to make the decisions they needed to make? He may have even said something like, "My job is to get out of your way." Within three days, however, he was asking to double-check the font you use in email correspondence because he was concerned that Courier New contradicted the innovation strategy that was tabled at the off-site. So much for freedom.

But working with constraints need not doom a creative endeavour. You just have to be mindful about allowing some room for yourself, or those you are working with, to use their imaginations, explore their new ideas and apply their creativity. Ron Tite had this kind of opportunity while working on the marketing campaign that launched the Volvo C30 in Canada.

While he was creative director at Euro RSCG, Ron's team picked up a global campaign that solicited consumer feedback with the tag line, "What do you think?" It was incredibly relevant, but the Toronto office wanted to complement it with something original for the Canadian market. They decided to open a pop-up art gallery in Toronto's trendy Queen West neighbourhood. They approached four DJs, four fashion designers and four artists for the program. They asked the artists what they thought of the car and offered to pay them to express that opinion through their chosen medium. The gallery would show the works for a month. One artist, one DJ and one fashion designer would share the gallery for one week so they could showcase their other work.

How did Ron's company convince the artists to engage in this commercial enterprise? And how could the agency ensure that the artwork that was completed was genuinely original and meaningful? When Ron gathered the artists in the boardroom to explain the initiative, he knew that to get them completely onside, he had to give them the ultimate freedom to truly express themselves. You can't pay someone for their opinion and then censor them when they honestly tell you what they think. He said, "We want you to express your opinion of the car. If you think that cars are killing the planet and that's what you want to communicate through your art, so be it. You have complete freedom to do what you want. We will not censor you, we will not ask to see your work beforehand and we will support you however we can through the process."

That's precisely what the artists needed to hear for the campaign to be successful, and precisely what the marketers needed to say.

In the end, one artist painted a cityscape. One painted a tornado using motor oil as the medium. One turned a real Volvo C30 into a camera obscura that projected the outside world onto photographic paper. The fourth artist shot a video of a day in the life of the car from the car's perspective and projected that video onto the hood of the car in the gallery. They were all wonderfully brilliant works of art that clients, partners, dealers and consumers absolutely loved. The artists stepped up as partners but remained true to their artistic vision.

Let's be honest, most of us have bosses at work. *All* of us have constraints in our personal and public lives. Complete freedom and control are usually illusory. It's no different for artists, but a true artist still has to be authentic. If there isn't a piece of their soul in their work, they're not artists.

Seth Godin, in his book *Linchpin: Are You Indispensable?*, seems to agree: "What makes someone an artist? I don't think it has anything to do with a paintbrush. There are painters who follow the numbers, or paint billboards or work in a small village in China painting reproductions. These folks, while swell people, aren't artists. On the other hand, Charlie Chaplin was an artist, beyond a doubt. So is Jonathan Ive, who designed the iPod. . . . An artist is someone who uses bravery, insight, creativity, and boldness to challenge the status quo. And an artist takes it personally."

Our favourite part is the last line. When your sweat and your soul are on the page or on the canvas, how can you not take it personally? How can you not defend the work that reveals your innermost thoughts and beliefs? If the work isn't an extension of yourself, you're not creating. You are simply producing. This essential originality and authenticity don't grow from sizing up the competition. Artists don't do consumer segmentation, SWOT analyses or business plans that identify opportunities in their category. As Ron likes to point out, no comedian examines other comics' material to identify bits that haven't been explored: *Well, airplane humour over-indexes in the stand-up scene, but there is a massive opportunity for material focused on broccoli, NASCAR and season 1 of* Glee. *Audiences identified those areas as relevant in quantitative research but few comedians are delivering against those insights.*

Of course not. Comedians write material that is based on their reactions to personal observations and is shaped by their personal beliefs and values. And while there may be shared styles and subjects, the best comedians have a take that is distinctly their own.

PERHAPS RIGHT ABOUT NOW, with all of this talk of authenticity and uniqueness, some readers might be thinking about the quotation that Steve Jobs made famous in 1996: "Good artists copy; great artists steal." (Jobs attributed the line to Picasso, but interestingly enough, it has been so often repeated in so many different variations that, if he indeed did say it, Picasso was both copying and stealing. The origin of this quote apparently goes back to a long-forgotten critic named W. H. Davenport Adams, who expressed the sentiment in a review of Tennyson's poetry in an 1892 edition of *The Gentleman's Magazine*.)

Being authentic and original does not mean creating something completely out of thin air. (Just for fun, we tried to think of a piece of art or an innovation of any kind that had absolutely no connection to anything else. After a while, we had to take some Advil and lie down.) All art, whether it is literature, painting, music or dance, is informed by what has gone before. Great art, however, brings something new to the enterprise. T. S. Eliot, in his own version of Davenport Adams's idea, explained that how poets change what they use can reveal who is a true great: "One of the surest of tests is the way in which a poet borrows. Immature poets imitate; mature poets steal; bad poets deface what they take, and good poets make it into something better, or at least something different. The good poet welds his theft into a whole of feeling which is unique, utterly different from that from which it was torn; the bad poet throws it into something which has no cohesion."

Many artists acknowledge their debts to others, but note that any sort of "borrowing" has to be approached with extreme caution. In his essay "How I Write," Bertrand Russell describes how in his early writing career, he was heavily influenced by the prose of John Milton: "His rolling periods reverberated through the caverns of my mind. I cannot say that I no longer admire them, but for me to imitate them involves a certain insincerity. In fact, all imitation is dangerous.... A style is not good unless it is an intimate and almost involuntary expression of the personality of the writer, and then only if the writer's personality is worth expressing."

And author François-René de Chateaubriand wrote, "The original writer is not he who refrains from imitating others, but he who can be imitated by none."

What these artists are getting at is that great artists and original thinkers rely upon what has gone before without simply recycling material or being derivative. Rather, they take ideas and build on them—use them to create new ideas and ventures, to make works that are truly their own.

This is, of course, true of all creative thinking, breakthroughs and innovation. Think of the scientific world. Scientists take into consideration all that is "known" about what they are interested in, in order to focus on what is unknown and yet to be discovered. When a scientist or a group of scientists publishes a finding, other scientists rush to reproduce the results in order to test the work. If a study shows promise, they will design their own experiments to refine and build on the discoveries. The scientific community may, however, ask questions about assumptions that have been made or conclusions that have been drawn. Sometimes scientists do reject theories or studies. But good scientists generally do this by responding with other evidence or theories—engaging in what is usually a productive intellectual debate. They don't reject advancements only because they are the work of the competition.

Just as in the arts and in the rest of life, competition exists in the scientific world—there is a limited amount of funding, a limited number of jobs and academic positions, a limited amount of space in scientific journals, a limited number of awards and acknowledgements. And there can be competitive nationalistic or philosophic agendas influencing the work. We only have to think of the American versus Soviet race to space. The national rivalry led to a huge number of scientific breakthroughs on both sides.

The important thing is that neither side rejected what was learned about breaking the sound barrier or metal fatigue or the effects of zero gravity on the human body, just because the "other side" had discovered it first. That sounds kind of obvious, doesn't it? But that didn't stop the German physics community during the Second World War from putting their own bizarre spin on scientific competition. This nationalist, pro-Nazi group rejected the idea that Jewish scientists (like Einstein) might be capable of good work, instead believing that the only true breakthroughs could come from "Aryan" scientists. With the encouragement and support of the Third Reich, they rejected "Jüdische Physik" in favour of "Deutsche Physik." Luckily for the Allied powers, this doomed Germany in the race to build a nuclear bomb. Yeah, competition works well in sports and shampoo sales. Physics, not so much.

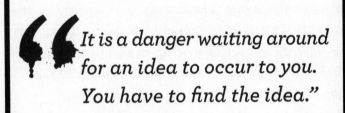 *It is a danger waiting around for an idea to occur to you. You have to find the idea."*

—Gerhard Richter, artist

So while you need to be authentic to maximize your creative potential and truly embrace creative thinking, this uniqueness does not mean that you have to be divorced from the thinking or the work that has gone before. You just have to make sure that you're indeed contributing something "new" to the endeavour.

Yet, there are always pitfalls to applying or realizing creative breakthroughs. As T. S. Eliot intimated, there's often a very fine line between "new" and "old," between "inspired" and "copying," between "individual" and absolutely everyone else. The first wave of hipsters devoted to thrift store fashion presented a unique look; today, however, there is such a shortage of slightly frayed flannel shirts and ironic tuques at the Goodwill that H&M and the Gap have had to rush in to fill the demand.

Innovation and creative solutions have to be handled carefully to preserve their importance and usefulness. In an excerpt from his book *Stand Out: Find Your Edge, Win at Work*, bestselling author and business consultant Marcus Buckingham points out that the challenge with innovations in work structures, procedures, management and so on is that what works well for one person does not necessarily work well for others. To be truly effective, an innovation has to be authentic to the individuals who use it. He notes, "At my company, TMBC, we have studied the country's best high school principals, the best affiliate leaders of Habitat for Humanity, the best emergency room nurses, the best pharmaceutical sales reps, and whenever we interview excellent performers in the same role, we find this same phenomenon—extraordinary results achieved in radically different ways." He goes on to caution leaders and companies against seeking a workplace innovation and then imposing it on everyone else. That doesn't end up being innovative—it ends up being "just another corporate program." At best, ineffective; at worst, foolish and awkward. Instead, he argues, workplace innovations should be applied selectively, offered only to the people for whom they are a good fit.

Okay, so authenticity and uniqueness make competition in artistic and creative efforts fairly meaningless. What should we take away from that? Why should we behave more like artists in this regard? Why should we reject or at least try to minimize competition when we are trying to think and work creatively?

Let's look at where most of us stand right now. So much of modern life has a competitive edge. In business and many other work environments, competition is endemic. As Amy C. Edmondson, professor of leadership and management at the Harvard Business School, puts it in "Get Rid of Unhealthy Competition":

> *Even when leaders don't explicitly paint a win-lose*
> *game for new recruits or new team members,*
> *the competitive mindset is essentially the default*
> *for most high-achieving professionals. It's*
> *overlearned in school. In every industry, those hired*

*by elite organizations have competed in endless
small contests along the way to achieve these
positions. This isn't bad in and of itself, of course.
But, the unintended consequence is a mindset
that views success as a zero-sum game, where my
success depends in part on your failure. This fosters
an inward focus, a focus on self—on how I'm doing
compared to others.*

She goes on to note that this kind of internal pressure causes people to become more concerned with the impression they are making than with what they can learn or how they might collaborate with others. In other words, the competitive environment can be the death knell of teamwork, and for creative thinking and idea generation.

Of course, the business world operates amid external competition too. We may spend our days worrying about market share or rival services or other innovative products that are going turn what we are making into the equivalent of eight-track tapes. But that has always been the way in the free market. Where the competition is *really* escalating is in our personal lives and our individual identities.

Keeping up with the Joneses used to be about what kind of car you had in the driveway or where you took your vacation. You might have been checking out your neighbour's renos or what schools your friends' kids were attending. None of that has gone away, but now technology, social media and the astounding new-found ability to share personal information have ramped up the comparisons. Who hasn't posted on Facebook and found themselves checking out how many "likes" they have gotten? (And wondering why our neighbour's photo of a sunset was more popular than the snap of our new barbecue pit.) Twitter lets us know how many followers we have, and just so that we don't get too smug about it, we can easily check how many *more* people follow that weird guy who works in the next office. Instagram seems to be about sharing pictures, but it can quickly feel like a "my photo album is better than your photo album" affair. And woe betide anyone who posts a video *anywhere* of their adorable toddler doing something amazingly precocious. We just dare you not to feel as if the very survival of said toddler depends on how many hits the video gets. (*Why the hell isn't this going viral yet? Don't people realize how damn cute it is?*)

Ah yes, in an era in which the humble brag has become ubiquitous, competition is leaking into almost everything we do. Even the mindful, spiritual art of stretching has fallen victim. In a January 2012 *New York Times Magazine* article entitled "How Yoga Can Wreck Your Body," William J. Broad described how yoga's explosion of popularity in the West has led to many classes being run by teachers who don't have the proper training and do not understand the practice. As a result, the emphasis on physical well-being has sometimes given way to a competitive edge worthy of an Olympic level sport. (Never mind the spiritual aspect, which is often completely MIA.) The race to turn ourselves into better pretzels than the pretzel on the mat next to us has led to serious injuries.

All of those ruined backs and aching hip joints are a good metaphor for the damage we do to our artistic selves when we let competition impinge on our creative efforts. Creative thinking is dependent on moving past distractions, on concentrating on *our own* thoughts and observations. Generating original ideas is almost impossible if we are constantly returning to what has been done before and worrying about how our ideas are going to stack up against someone else's. Feeling competitive while trying to creatively work, plan or solve problems gets in the way of coming up with unique, authentic ideas.

The flip side is that just like artists, if we maintain our unique, authentic focus, we actually make competition impossible—or at least hollow and pointless. What we produce is unlikely to be exactly the same as someone else's material. And our efforts have a much greater chance of being judged on their own merits and valued for their own strengths.

There's a great European spot for the Smart Car that we love because it embraces how being unique moves us past the competition. The spot opens with a familiar car ad trope: the Smart Car is racing down a dirt road. But as the ad progresses it becomes clear that the little car is not quite up to the demands of a rugged, open-terrain marketing pitch. It gets stuck going up a gravel hill. It almost topples over when it attempts to drive over a boulder. It stalls in the middle of a stream, its little windshield wipers flapping away helplessly. Clearly, when it comes to off-roading, the Smart Car sucks. But the last shot is the most important. It shows a large Suburban/Escalade/military-sized SUV slowing down but eventually passing a small parking spot. The Smart Car follows, scoots in and parks without a problem.

Clearly, if you want to take your car to the desert, the Smart Car is not the vehicle for you. But if you want to get around town quickly and park with ease, the Smart Car is your ride. Its manufacturers make no apologies for their tiny product—they're confident in its unique abilities.

While it may be easy to understand why constant comparison and competition in our personal lives is a bad idea (several reports have now come out claiming that Facebook is actually contributing to depression and your feeling lousy about yourself), it can be challenging to see why it would be problematic in business or professional life. But true creativity means bringing something new and fresh to the enterprise, which simply can't happen if you are spending all of your energy thinking about the "competition" or about what others are doing.

Take, for example, Apple and Microsoft. Their competition and liberal stealing and borrowing from each other have been the stuff of countless books, news reports and legal battles. But both have managed to "win" various competitions by putting aside what the other or their competitors are doing.

It's hard to remember that there was anything before the iPod. But there was. In fact, there were a number of different MP3 players out there, but you can be forgiven for forgetting who made them or what they looked like. Suffice it to say, they were different shapes and sizes, but all of them worked essentially the same way, and all required you to hunt down your own music from a few online services or your old CD collection, and copy and transfer them to your device.

When Steve Jobs ventured into the music business, he decided to put all of that aside and start fresh. He saw the utility of the core concept, but took a step back from what was currently being tried to concentrate on the total music experience. That meant not just having a huge amount of music on a small device; it also meant how you bought that music, how you stored it and how you accessed it. He aimed for ease. He wanted it to be intuitive. He knew that it should appeal to everyone—after all, music fans certainly aren't limited to techies or early adopters.

So the iPod he developed was the very definition of simplicity—just four buttons, which were quickly replaced by a single dial. But almost more important was the whole ecosystem surrounding the device. It came with iTunes, a simple and intuitive music manager, and two years later, Apple launched the iTunes store, a vast library it had compiled by striking first-of-their-kind business deals with all of the major music publishers. The monolithic iTunes meant that you could find, buy and transfer just about every kind of music—thousands and thousands of songs—with a few keystrokes on your computer. And plugging your iPod into your computer was the only thing you had to do to fill the thing with music. The experience did feel completely different. And it left the rest of the MP3 business in ashes.

(Interestingly, Microsoft tried to follow suit with the Zune—a device that was to become the Edsel of the portable music industry, so spectacular was its failure. The funny thing about the Zune was that it was an extremely capable MP3 player with numerous innovations, one of which was remarkably prescient: a music subscription service, which was the precursor to the now enormously successful businesses like Spotify, Apple Music and Google Play. But despite that unique feature, it simply couldn't escape the popular perception that it was a pale imitation of an iPod.)

Jobs continued the kind of success he enjoyed with the iPod by rethinking cellphones. By taking a step back from the clunky keyboards and ugly operating systems of precursor smartphones like Blackberry and Windows Mobile, he was able to bring the usefulness of a Web-connected pocket computer to the masses. With a sleek touchscreen and user interface whose intuitive simplicity belied its functional power, Apple launched a product that completely revolutionized computing as we know it today.

The various Apple successes seem to have taught Microsoft a thing or two. Realizing that it was falling behind in the tablet and the PC market in general, Microsoft abandoned any idea of tinkering with an iPad rival (there would be no "ZunePad"). Instead, it tried to focus on what the future of computing might look like. The results were the extremely successful Surface line, which combines the full power of a laptop with the features of a tablet and the size of a notebook. It is also developing Holo-Lens, a personal hologram technology, which—although in its early stages—by all accounts looks poised to be a truly innovative breakthrough that could be to the smartphone what the smartphone was to the traditional PC.

Apple CEO Tim Cook in an NBC interview in December 2012 summarized the mindset that both companies now seem to have embraced: "The reality is, is that we love competition at Apple. We think it makes us all better. But we want people to invent their own stuff."

On a smaller scale, internal competition within an organization is also counterproductive to creativity. In an interview with *Fast Company* magazine, Teresa Amabile, head of the Entrepreneurial Management Unit at Harvard Business School, had this to say about workplace competition: "There's a widespread belief, particularly in the finance and high-tech industries, that internal competition fosters innovation. In our surveys, we found that creativity takes a hit when people in a work group compete instead of collaborate. The most creative teams are those that have the confidence to share and debate ideas. But when people compete for recognition, they stop sharing information. And that's destructive because nobody in an organization has all of the information required to put all the pieces of the puzzle together.

As we discussed in Chapter 3, the campus approach that has become so popular among tech companies is designed precisely to encourage the sharing information and the cross-pollination of ideas.

Thinking more creatively and being innovative can clearly be driven by competition. But the work itself, the idea generation and the product development, is most successful when it stops focusing on the competitors' products or practices. True innovation, like art, is not just tinkering with someone else's ideas.

We used to say that a little competition never hurt anyone. In the general scheme of things, that's probably true: competition can make us better. But inspiration can be more powerful. There's nothing wrong with benchmarking others' successes. (Artists can be inspired by other's successes after all.) But it's important that we put competition in its place and not let it distract us from being our most creative selves.

It's good to wean yourself off that particular narcotic [praise]. You cannot control what other people say and you cannot make people like you. So you've got to do what you want."

—John Mulaney, comedian

HUSH THE HATERS (INCLUDING THE ONE INSIDE YOUR HEAD)

Meryl Streep tells a great story about what we would call a "hater." She was auditioning for a role in *King Kong* when she was in her twenties, she told Graham Norton during a 2015 appearance on his talk show in the U.K. Dino De Laurentiis's son had seen the young Meryl in a play and brought her in to meet his father. Dino Sr. took one look at Streep, turned to his son, and said in Italian, "Why do you bring me this ugly thing?" (Charming fellow, that De Laurentiis.)

Little did the director know that Streep spoke Italian and understood every word of the blistering sting. She replied in Italian, "I'm sorry I'm not beautiful enough to be in *King Kong*." As she tells the story to Norton, Streep's tone is withering and she laughs about her inability to play a convincing love interest to an enormous ape. But she also says that the rejection was "very sobering for a young girl." No kidding! If De Laurentiis wasn't a hater, we're not sure who would be.

The term *hater* is relatively new, but the people sure aren't. They are not necessarily as nasty as De Laurentiis was. They probably don't hate you or what you are doing. But they are the people around you—co-workers, friends, even loved ones—who criticize you, or dismiss your ideas, or squelch your enthusiasm with a well-timed sigh or a raised eyebrow. Sometimes they simply ignore you and your ideas. And while we have all experienced this human incarnation of a cold shower, when it comes to negativity and those who like to spread it around, celebrities draw haters like industrial-strength magnets. If you need any proof (or are looking for a little entertaining work-avoidance), check out Jimmy Kimmel's "Celebrities Read Mean Tweets" (about themselves) on YouTube. Some of the comments are enough to make you wonder if decency should be designated an endangered species.

But even if they aren't celebrities, everyone in the entertainment business knows about the haters. In her book *Is Everyone Hanging Out Without Me?*, TV writer, director, producer and actor Mindy Kaling talks about the heavyweight doubters she and her friend Brenda Withers faced at the very start of their careers, when putting together their first TV show. The two had previously written a quirky comedic play called *Matt & Ben*, which imagined the friendship and circumstances that led up to Matt Damon and Ben Affleck's movie hit *Good Will Hunting*. Mindy played Ben; Bren played Matt. The show was a runaway off-Broadway hit, garnering rave reviews in the *New Yorker* and the *New York Times* and from just about every theatre critic who warmed a seat in the small theatres in which it played. It even caught the attention of TV execs from a major network. Mindy and Bren were asked to develop a sitcom about, essentially, themselves—two young women, just starting their careers in NYC. The show would even be called "Mindy and Bren." It sounded like a dream gig. Except it wasn't.

Mindy and Bren were supposed to write the pilot, but the studio produced a laundry list of trendy products and issues they wanted worked into the story somehow. It was a recipe for a sitcom that was about as hilarious as a pan of date squares. But at least the women knew that they had a couple of genuinely funny actors to breathe some life into it—themselves. That's where things got really weird. The network execs quickly dismissed Mindy and Bren's naive assumption: they would have to *audition* for the roles. In other words, they would have to compete with other actors to play *themselves*.

"This is how I found out," writes Mindy Kaling, "that I could convincingly play Ben Affleck but not Mindy Kaling." Neither of them got the part.

Much to Kaling's relief, the pilot, based on script crippled with product placements and contemporary non-sequiturs, never got picked up. She didn't have to watch another person doing a better job of being Mindy than she did.

Of course, the work of all actors, based as it is on auditions, is rife with rejection and criticism. Canadian actress Sheila McCarthy is, by any measure, a success. Working steadily in the industry since her teens, she's had hundreds of roles, won numerous awards, starred in an indie hit (*I've Heard the Mermaids Singing*), and acted in blockbuster movies and TV series, north and south of the border. Over the course of her career, however, she estimates that she's done well over two thousand auditions. Just do the math on that one. It translates into an awful lot of rejection.

But actors aren't the only artists who are buffeted by negativity. Most, in fact, are. There are thousands of people who make their living by delivering withering reviews (as well as the occasional morsel of praise) of artistic and creative works. For example, here's what Gia Kourlas, writing in *Time Out New York*, had to say about dancer Sylvie Guillem's *6,000 Miles Away*: "Even if you think Guillem still has it (or ever did) this overhyped, horrid evening of dance was typical of the mediocre crap coming out of Sadler's Wells." Alex Ross, writing in the *New Yorker*, decried the current state of opera, providing as an example Robert Lepage's production of Wagner's

The Ring Cycle at the Met: "Pound for pound, ton for ton, it is the most witless and wasteful production in modern operatic history."

But even works that have gone on to become bona fide successes haven't escaped the pointy tip of the critics' blade. (Bill Henderson and Pushcart Press published an entire series of books called *Rotten Reviews* to collect these barbs aimed at literary writers and their work.) In 1855, the *London Critic* reviewed *Leaves of Grass*, pronouncing, "Whitman is as unacquainted with art as a hog is with mathematics." The *New York Times Book Review* dropped this little bomb on Joseph Heller's *Catch-22*: "It gasps for want of craft and sensibility." And one publisher, on receiving John le Carré's first novel, *The Spy Who Came in from the Cold*, pronounced, "Le Carré . . . hasn't got a future."

Anyone who puts any writing, thoughts or work of any kind out into the world is likely to get some negative feedback. The arrival of the Internet has pretty much guaranteed this—the Web is an enormous never-ending playground for haters and "trolls." (Just spend a little time in the comments section of any YouTube video if you have an especially high tolerance for vitriol and bad spelling.) The ease with which anyone can slag anything these days has made some publications rethink their approach to the comments sections of their online offerings altogether. Take a look at the *Globe and Mail* or *New York Times* or *Forbes* magazine. In the margin around most news and opinion pieces is a little tab that says "comments."

You have to click it to read the comments or write one, right? But that wasn't always the case. In the early days of online magazines and newspapers, the comments sections often immediately followed the articles. This meant that a long, thoughtful piece on public education, or a heavily researched article on supply-side economics, or even, say, an urgent news alert about an impending weather front would often be immediately followed by something along the lines of *"What a load of crap!"—Carl B., Uxbridge, ON.* It was a bizarre and disconcerting way to end the reading experience. And the journalists who laboured on the articles weren't too pleased either. Editorial boards everywhere decided to create a little breathing room between the journalistic offerings and the critiques—cranky or otherwise.

Even in the tech world, that hub of creative thinking and innovation, the doubters and naysayers lurk everywhere. Jakob Porsér, the co-founder of Minecraft, describes how he first reacted to Markus Persson's blocky, crude-looking new video game: "I was like, 'It's good you're keeping busy.'" Apparently a number of Persson's other friends also responded to the game with less enthusiasm than if he had shown them his plans for video version of tic-tac-toe.

Mark Zuckerberg has also been surrounded by a chorus of grumpy critics since he launched Facebook. Tech journalist Harry McCracken sums up the hate: "Facebook wouldn't work outside Harvard. It wouldn't work outside elite colleges. It wouldn't work among the general populace. It couldn't topple MySpace. It couldn't make enough money to justify its valuation. It couldn't hold on to teen-agers once their parents signed up. It wouldn't matter as much on smartphones as it had on PCs. It couldn't make enough money on mobile to satisfy Wall Street."

And remember our discussion of Twitter and its embrace of the "unrealistic" in Chapter 3? Well, that little piece of innovation certainly didn't escape the haters. Three years after Twitter launched, the *New York Times* even ran a blog post that asked readers "Do You Still Think Twitter Is Stupid?" These are some of the responses that inquiry produced:

- "Twitter is a joke. Any business that thinks it will somehow help to post tweets is nuts. Please put your energy to use in figuring out new markets— not stupid time-wasting microblogging." (Zorro1x)
- Twitter has limited value in special situations at most. For others it [is] worthless. There is good reason 90% of those who sign up stop using it within one month. Including myself . . . Twitter is a fad more than anything else." (AH2)
- "Yes, Twitter is mostly still stupid! Think about how much wasted time there is on this site. Obvi-ously it is useful for getting the word out from Iran or breaking news in real time. But who really cares about 99.999% of the junk on there?" (Stephen Robert Morse)

- "Twitter is the PointCast of the 21st century—an interesting novelty today, but destined to go the way of the 95LX, the Netscape browser and the Furby." (Tom)

Okay, you get the picture. These days, we all face a lot of haters. And interestingly enough, despite all the lip service companies and society pay to the importance of creative thinking, research has shown that anyone attempting to work and think out of the box is likely to be told to crawl right back in. And the hating starts early.

Two studies conducted in the 1990s by Erik L. Westby and V. L. Dawson (and published in the *Creativity Research Journal*) looked at how teachers responded to the creativity of their elementary school students. Students were first rated for their creative abilities by the researchers. Then the teachers (without being shown the creativity rankings) were asked to rate which students were their favourites. It probably won't surprise anyone who has been told to stop doodling in class or had "This was not the assignment!" scrawled across their work that those who were ranked "least favourite" had scored the highest on the creativity assessments—and vice versa. And this despite the fact that the teachers claimed to enjoy working with creative children. Westby and Dawson did a second study in which the teachers were asked to come up with their own concepts of creativity. Perhaps not surprisingly, these did not look exactly the same as those developed by the research team. But perhaps the most interesting thing about this second test was that while the teachers' rankings of the students now lined up a little more closely with the creativity rankings, it wasn't a strong correlation.

Psychologist Maria Konnikova explains, in *Mastermind: How to Think Like Sherlock Holmes,* that people may be wired to have an unconscious distrust of creativity and creative ideas. She reports that Jennifer Mueller, a University of San Diego School of Business professor, has redesigned Harvard University's Implicit Association Test, a test that measures the gap between our conscious and unconscious attitudes, to gauge our reactions to creative ideas:

> *The result indicated that even those people who had explicitly ranked creativity as high on their list of positive attributes showed an implicit bias against it relative to practicality under conditions of uncertainty. And what's more, they also rated an idea that had been pretested as creative (for example, a running shoe that uses nanotechnology to adjust fabric thickness to cool the foot and reduce blisters) as less creative than their more certain counterparts. So not only were they implicitly biased, but they exhibited a failure to see creativity for what it was when directly faced with it.*

Sure, the experiment looked at how individuals made decisions in "uncertain conditions," but doesn't that description cover most of life?

So while mean-spirited tweeters might target Julia Roberts's teeth, even those of us who are doing what we were asked to do in that "innovation" seminar we had to attend for work are likely to hear from haters once we share our creative efforts.

Stories of misguided haters, tone-deaf reviewers or critics who possess a remarkable lack of prescience can be a lot of fun. Who doesn't like to think of these guys watching the artists or innovators they dissed pick up awards, receive enormous paycheques and bask in public adoration. But the important point is not that the haters got it wrong. It's that the artists and creators got it right. And they did that by hushing the haters.

Meryl Streep didn't stop going to auditions, Mindy Kaling didn't stop acting, and John le Carré didn't stop writing. Markus Persson didn't walk away from Minecraft, and Biz Stone didn't let the negativity affect his plans for Twitter. (As Biz said, "You have to love what you do and that was the case with Twitter because everyone was telling us how stupid it was.")

And most important, none of these artists or innovators let the haters move into their heads permanently or let the negativity feed their own inner critics. As art critic Sarah Thornton has said about artists, "Contemporary art . . . requires intense self-belief."

That's probably the most important message here. The problem with paying too much attention to the boss who dismisses your suggestion, or the co-worker who questions the way you do things, or the family member who tries to dissuade you from trying something new is that all of these negative responses tend to bolster whatever self-doubt you already possess. (And some of us already have enough to fill a good-sized storage locker.) And self-doubt stokes fear.

As we will discuss in the next chapter, fear has its uses when we are trying to expand our thinking and break free from the same-old, same-old. But it can also, obviously, inhibit creativity. It makes us play it safe, return to traditional and commonly accepted ideas and practices—just like we saw in the fork, knife, butter discussion in Chapter 3. Stephen King sees this as one of the biggest challenges for writers: "I'm convinced," he says in his Top 20 Rules for Writers, "that fear is at the root of most bad writing."

The inner censor we all have is not an ally when we are trying to open ourselves up to new ways of thinking and seeing. In other words, just like artists, everyone needs "intense self-belief," at least from time to time. Embarking on any new or creative venture, whether it's launching a business, trying a unique teaching method or rethinking the way you manage your blended family requires a certain level of confidence.

But hushing the haters is about more than developing a Teflon-coated ego and barrelling ahead. If that's your sole approach, you may be entering the realm of magical thinking—where you end up on *America's Got Talent* warbling painfully off-key to an Adele song. The best way to hush the haters is to find ways to use the negativity in a constructive way.

One approach is to recognize that there is something inherently positive about negativity. The artists that we spoke to at the Art Battle described in the previous chapter professed loving the "hate" they sometimes received. Or at least they would prefer to have someone hate their work than think it was just *okay*. Many said they would rather someone was offended or disgusted than completely unmoved. And that's because they know that when people hate a piece of art, they are engaged. It's not that the piece doesn't speak to them; it's that the piece screams at the top of its lungs, "I am definitely not the work for that space above your couch! Buy me and your spouse will have you evaluated!" When we generate ideas or works of art, we are hoping to get responses—and when someone hates something, we not only get a reaction, we also hear the passion in that response.

But there's more to the artists' love of hate than that. What the artists we talked to found liberating was the knowledge that for every hate, there was often an equal and opposite love. They were seeking the enthusiasm of their true fans, knowing full well that the cost of doing so was alienating those who weren't fans. And they were okay with that.

Many artists go even further and actually find ways to use the negativity to spur *more* creativity. Ron's experience as a stand-up comedian has led him to think about haters as either active and inactive hecklers. And he has come up with ways of dealing with both.

For a comedian, active hecklers are those (often inebriated) audience members who want to provide real-time feedback on the material you've spent days or weeks preparing. They shout from the back, talk loudly to the people around them and generally try to steal the spotlight by providing additional jokes. While active hecklers are an occupational hazard for comics, they make an appearance in everyone's lives. Their online counterparts are Internet trolls. When the active heckler is a troll, you just have to ignore them. It's pointless to engage with someone who is energized by your escalating responses. (Don't feed the troll; let it starve to death. In the online world, you need to limit your discussions to the people who provide relatively sound and intelligent arguments or queries, and respond to them with logical and data-proven responses of your own.)

But active hecklers might also be those people in a meeting or a presentation who interrupt to offer up picayune corrections or superfluous information. They may be your co-workers with the "no-can-do" spirit—the people who can see the downside to every workplace change or new business strategy. Or they may be those family members who always find a reason why things have to be done their way.

If you are face to face, you have to deal with an active heckler. If you're a singer, you have to get the room back. If you're in a presentation, you have to get the meeting back. If you're at home, you have to get the remote back.

Regardless, the only way to deal with the active heckler is to engage the heckler. That may mean thanking someone for their contribution and moving on quickly. It may mean providing additional support for or clarification of your ideas. Or it may mean acknowledging the critique and promising to do additional work or research to address the concerns. The important thing is to use the challenges to strengthen and improve your plans or ideas rather than allowing them to spell the end of your efforts.

Perhaps trickier is dealing with the inactive heckler. Is there anything worse for a comedian than having someone stand on his chair in the middle of their set and yell out at the top of his alcohol-infused lungs, "You suuuuuck!"?

Yes, Ron assures us, there is. Worse than the active heckler is the inactive one: the person who doesn't even realize you're on stage.

While hearing and having to respond to active hecklers can be a soul-destroying experience (or insanely irritating at the very least), it's not nearly as bad as playing to a room that isn't even aware you're in it, a room where the jokes you've worked on for weeks can't be heard over the sounds of drinks being ordered and bar mates debating the merits of mixed martial arts.

Of course, this doesn't just happen to stand-up comics. You've probably been in one of those meetings where your detailed sales strategy or thoughts on the new curriculum seem to be just so much white noise to the colleague check-ing her email, or the fellow next to her working on his own presentation, or the guy flipping through the handouts looking for what? The cartoons? Even worse are the people who may be physically present but are mentally mapping the best route to get to their kid's T-ball game on time. These folks may not be verbally heckling, but they're mentally heckling.

Discussion is, after all, a good thing. As with brainstorming, feedback and debate are positive because they can help you improve your ideas. They can also help to remove doubts, overcome challenges and get the confident approvals you need to move forward. A lack of dialogue often means that people don't care, or if they do, they'd rather not voice why they don't like what you're saying. That's dangerous (and may mean that your ideas are going to receive a death blow a few hours later in hallway discussion by the powers-that-be). So what should you do about those inactive hecklers?

Dealing with inactive hecklers is actually rather simple. You just need to convert them into active hecklers so you can engage them and address any concerns directly. You need to get them to listen and press them for their opinion even if you don't think it'll be a positive one. In other words, force them to heckle so you can respond.

Ron explains how he managed to do this at one of his comedy performances:

I once did a show at a bar called the Chick'n'Deli,
which was famous for its live music on Sunday

nights. *The first time they decided to preface the live bands with live comedy, I was asked to headline. Performing in non-comedy bars isn't my idea of fun, but I knew the host and the rest of the lineup, so, begrudgingly, I agreed.*

*The crowd wasn't there to see comedy, and they weren't exactly supportive of delaying the music for a completely different form of entertainment. The host didn't pick up on this critical piece of feedback, and instead of working to get them onside, chose to use blue material that only fuelled their displeasure. It's amazing how the repeated use of the word "motherf****r" turns people off.*

Within seconds, we had lost them. They turned their backs on the stage and began talking to one another. The entire room had a buzz of conversation while the comics struggled to deliver their material above the noise.

As he was preparing to introduce me, the host incorporated some additional inappropriate material that delivered the final blow. As he wrapped up, I heard one lone patron at the back of the room spit out, "You're an asshole." The host's response? "Well, you're a [bleep]ing cougar. Please welcome your headliner, Ron Tite."

Lovely. As I got to the stage, there was no

applause to welcome me. There was no break in the conversation, either. I could have been Richard Pryor reincarnated, and they wouldn't have noticed. It didn't matter what material I selected because they weren't going to hear it anyhow. I had to get them onside, but to do that, I needed them to know that I was there.

I started with a story: "I was walking down the street the other day and I walked into that store. Uh, that store whose name is, uh . . ."

I stammered and pretended that I completely forgot a key reference in my material. I acted as if I was panicked about my memory loss and gave them clues so they could help me out. "You know the store owned by those two guys. It's the one with the beaver on their sweatshirts." After ten seconds of silence, someone offered, "Roots?"

That's when it began to change. The crowd who was previously distracted were now beginning to pay attention because they thought they were going to witness a train wreck happen right before their very eyes.

"Yes, Roots. Thanks. Anyway, I wanted to try on these shoes, and the salesperson reached into his shirt pocket and pulled out a . . . a . . . uh . . ." I purposely blanked again, but this time, they didn't have enough information to be able to guess what

the correct answer was. I continued, "Uh . . . Um . . . he took out a uh . . ."

That's when the conversation stopped. The room fell silent and the crowd turned to face the stage. They wanted to see the horror that was happening before them. I simply waited. I wasn't going to proceed before someone in the audience made a suggestion.

"He took out a . . . Oh, what do you call that thing? Uh . . ."

Finally, after thirty of the most uncomfortable seconds in my life, a man near the front guessed, "Pen?"

"Yes, pen. He took out a pen and started to sign a piece of paper because he assumed I wanted his autograph. That's when I realized that the sales guy at Roots was actually that famous Canadian actor, uh . . . what's his name?"

"William Shatner?"

"Yeah. William Shatner. I thought, 'Wow, how Canadian does this store have to be that they summon Captain Kirk to help me buy a leather brogue?'" I launched into a bad William Shatner impersonation, but it didn't matter. They knew that the story was being driven by their suggestions, and before long, they were challenging me with odd suggestions like "didgeridoo" and "Madge from the Palmolive commercials" just *to see how I would incorporate them into the narrative.*

I don't even remember how the story ended, but it didn't matter. I concluded the audience participation segment and launched into the material that I had planned to use all along. My set went as well as any other I had done. They laughed in all the right places and by the end of the night appeared to have thoroughly enjoyed themselves.

In other settings, turning the inactive heckler into an active heckler might mean asking for the opinion of someone who is suspiciously quiet at a meeting. It may be inviting a cellphone checker to help you explain a point you tried to make during a presentation. It could mean assigning the biggest critic of a project to join the development team (or the most disruptive student in the class to lead an activity). It might be asking your fussy-eater kids to come up with their own dinner ideas—which you can teach them to cook for the whole family. The point is to force the heckler from silence to feedback that you might be able to use.

While dealing with hecklers, inactive and active, can feel like an annoying waste of time, it's good to remember that we actually *need* critics. Novelist Zadie Smith has gone so far as to say that writers need to be their own haters. One of the 10 Rules for Writing that she composed for the *Guardian* newspaper recommended that writers "try to read their own work as a stranger would read it, or even better, as an enemy would." So while we don't want those internal censors to shut down the show, we do need to listen to them. But it's all about timing when it comes to our internal review staff. British musician Fyfe Dangerfield puts it this way: "We all have that small voice that tells us we're rubbish, and we need to learn when to silence it. Early in the songwriting process, comparisons do nothing but harm: sometimes I put on a David Bowie record and think, 'Why do I bother?' But when it comes to recording or mixing, you do need to be your own critic and editor. It's a bit like having children: you don't interfere with the birth, but as your child grows up, you don't let it run wild."

The story of the 2013 Banff Centre for the Fine Arts photo essay competition illustrates the importance of unleashing this internal critic at the appropriate point in the creative process.

Every year, the Banff Centre holds an international photo essay competition. The general topic is wildlife or wilderness. To be considered a photo essay rather than simply a collection of photos of a particular place, group or event, the photographer must tell a story. The photo essay must, as a whole, share meaning, a meaning that is more than the sum of its parts.

For many years, the competition has been flooded with entries. New technologies, including the high-quality cameras in our phones, have made taking photos a hugely popular activity. In 2013, the panel of judges, which included author and journalist Ian Brown, considered a total of over five hundred entries. They agreed that many of the photos were beautiful and engaging. But there was one problem. Not one of the submissions, each of which consisted of several photos, had any narrative structure. Brown and his co-judges felt the photos were not photo essays, but rather collections of photos on a single topic. The judges refused to issue the award. Ian Brown later wrote in the *Globe and Mail*:

> *Human beings have taken an estimated 3.5 trillion photographs since the first snapshot, of a Paris street, appeared in 1838. As many as 20 per cent were uploaded in the past two years. Why are most of them so forgettable?*
>
> *Even the entries that were remotely in the neighbourhood of telling a story—and most were hopelessly lost—were edited incomprehensibly. (Not experimentally. Incomprehensibly.) In other words, the best photographic sequences taken by amateur and professional wilderness photographers alike had no perceptible story, and therefore no significance.*
>
> *If my recent experience as a judge in an international photography competition is any evidence, our jones for digital photography is—with rare exceptions—a form of neurotic masturbation, fuelled by an unstoppable sense of technological entitlement.*

Brown and his fellow judges received a lot of flak for their decision. And whether or not you agree with it, they made an interesting point. Technology has allowed these photographers to capture beautiful, evocative images, but perhaps has also allowed them to put less thought into what they are doing with the camera. Before the advent of digital cameras, most of us would have twenty-four, at most thirty-six frames in our camera. Every poorly composed or badly lit photo cost us both in film and in developing fees. Photojournalists, especially war photographers, were even more restricted. Even if their employers were picking up the cost of film and developing, the photographers could only bring so many rolls of film with them when out in the field. They simply couldn't afford to waste frames. Faced with these constraints, good photographers snapped pictures that were the result of intense observation, artistic judgment and a critical eye. Their internal photo editors were involved in the creative process.

So while new technology allows us to engage in creative behaviours with considerable ease, it does not necessarily encourage us to hone our creativity. And that is a shame.

OUR INTERNAL CRITICS ARE important, but so too are those external critics—even the most negative ones. Tara Mohr, in her book *Playing Big: Find Your Voice, Your Mission, Your Message*, stresses the importance of others' reactions to our work, but she encourages us to put what we hear in context. Creator of the acclaimed Playing Big leadership program for women, Mohr argues that feedback doesn't tell us anything about ourselves, our ideas or our work. Instead, it tells us about those giving the feedback. But Mohr is quick to point out that this doesn't mean that feedback shouldn't have meaning for us:

> *Feedback is wildly important. . . . Feedback shouldn't be dismissed because it doesn't tell you anything about you. Feedback is vital not because it tells us about our own value but because it tells us whether we are reaching the people we need to reach.*
>
> *If an entrepreneur wants her pitch to be effective with venture investors, she needs to hear their feedback in order to learn what inspires them to invest. If an aspiring memoirist wants her work to be read widely, she needs to hear feedback from her intended audience. If a teacher wants her students to learn a lot and enjoy her class, she needs to know—from their feedback—whether that's happening.*
>
> *When you look at feedback this way, you can approach it with a kind of exquisite calm and centeredness because you know it's just useful data, nothing more. Feedback is not meant to give you self-esteem boosts or wounds. That's not its*

*place. It is meant to give you tactical information
about how to reach the people you want to reach.
Feedback is emotionally neutral information that
tells you what resonates for your desired audience,
what engages the people you want to engage, what
influences the people you want to influence.*

With Mohr's approach, you can maintain your confidence while encouraging and using feedback—no matter how negative it might be. But as you may have noticed, Mohr is talking about feedback from the people you want to engage with your ideas or creations—whether that's your audience, your clients, your co-workers, your family or your friends. As Ron recognized when he had to open for the music evening, if you aim your ideas at the wrong audience, you're likely going to end up hearing from the haters. You can use that experience, but if you really want to improve and grow, you also need the honest response of the people you want to address.

Finding those supportive critics isn't always easy. Friends and family are the obvious go-to people for many things, but you have to be careful. Your friends may consider their roles to be ones of love and support—we're here for you buddy, even if we are going to go home later and tell our partners how whacked your ideas really are. Your parents may think that everything you do is wonderful—after all, you're their offspring, how could it possibly be otherwise? Or they may feel that anything short of a sure bet is a risk they don't want to see any of their children taking. Either way, none of these responses is going to give you the kind of challenging feedback that will help you reach your potential.

You also have to be careful about looking to clients, audiences and co-workers for useful feedback. As anyone who has ever had a client will know, even the most brilliant proposals may face client pushback ("too expensive," "we've never done that before," "please don't suggest we change anything—just make things better"). Clients often balk at providing helpful feedback when you are being paid to generate the ideas, and it's easy for them to lose confidence in your abilities if they are presented with an idea that is not fully worked out. Indeed, audiences of any kind generally don't want to pay to help you beta-test a rough draft (hence reduced-rate theatre workshops and previews).

You need to be careful in choosing co-workers to give you feedback as well. While many of the most successful companies work in a collegial manner, we're sure that more than a few of you have had first-hand experiences with those other workplace "teams"—the ones that have more in common with *Survivor* or *Lord of the Flies* than with Silicone Valley's corporate campus approach. Co-workers may see your success as a threat to their own. They may resent taking time away from their own areas of responsibility to help you with yours (even if the end results will benefit everyone). They may see any changes to products or processes as more work for them.

Like the artists who formed circles like the Bloomsbury

Group and the Algonquin Round Table, mentioned in Chapter 3, you need to search out like minds that can be both honest and supportive. Those supportive critics need to be engaged with what you are saying. They need to *understand* what you are saying. They need to be willing to spend the time thinking about your work and forming their opinions of it. And they need to be willing and able to share those honest assessments with you. (As Tesla and SpaceX founder Elon Musk has said of supportive critics, "They know what's wrong with your product. You need to get it out of them.")

They also have to be comfortable with the fact that you may not always follow their advice or respond to their critiques.

At the heart of all these requirements is trust—you have to trust the person to be open and honest with you; they have to trust that they can share their opinions without damaging their relationship with you. It may take time to find these people, but it's worth it.

It would be easy to think of this chapter as simply one of those cheesy motivational posters that say something like, "Don't let the turkeys get you down!" But dealing with negative criticism needs to be more than ignoring what you don't like to hear. Simply humming loudly every time someone points out a flaw or weakness in what you are doing is to miss a great opportunity to improve. What you need to do is hush the haters by not allowing the negativity to squash your creative thinking or distract you from exploring your ideas fully. You need to think about whether their challenges are points that you can use to refine and improve your projects, and if they are, you need to incorporate them into the next stage of your plans. If the negativity is in the form of silence, you need to find ways to give it voice. And you need to generate feedback from people other than haters—from those who opinions you trust and value.

Hush the haters. Deal with the hecklers. Listen to feedback. And pay attention to your own internal critic. It's all part of being a creative thinker.

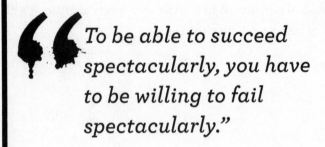 *To be able to succeed spectacularly, you have to be willing to fail spectacularly."*

—Biz Stone, Twitter co-founder

FLIP THE FLOP

A number of years ago, art historians and scientists decided to look at Picasso's famous *The Blue Room* with an infrared camera. For decades, experts had suspected that there might be something under this early painting of a woman bathing while standing in the centre of a small tub. (The texture of the paint seems to differ from area to area on the canvas.) The resulting imagery revealed that under the melancholy scene was a completely *different* melancholy painting (it was Picasso's "Blue Period" after all). This one was a close-up portrait of a glum-looking man in a bow tie, his head propped up on his hand.

There have been plenty of examples of artists revising and perfecting their works. Picasso himself apparently drew about forty-five preliminary sketches for his master-piece *Guernica*. And a microscopic study of a seascape by the Dutch master Hendrick van Anthonissen has shown that he painted out a huge beached whale that was originally at the centre of the work. (Perhaps van Anthonissen had decided to abandon his plans for a "dead things on the beach" series.) But what might be a little startling for some is that Picasso both abandoned his earlier work and *destroyed* it.

And this was not the only time. If you look carefully at *The Old Guitarist*, you can see the image of a woman's face that has been painted over behind the guitarist's neck. Van Gogh is also known to have wiped out some of his work. X-rays have shown that under his painting *Patch of Grass* is a head-and-shoulders portrait of a woman.

It is entirely likely that both van Gogh and Picasso painted over other pictures as a cost-saving measure—they simply couldn't afford new canvases. But it is probably safe to assume that they chose to erase works that they didn't care about, that they felt were not their best work or were flat-out failures.

Given that today you could sell a van Gogh grocery list or a parking ticket issued to Picasso for enough money to fund your retirement, it's hard to fathom that any of the paintings were erased. But it's proof that artists, just like the rest of us, produce stuff that they or others deem not up to snuff. But that really shouldn't surprise us. Picasso created over fifty thousand works of art. Many are considered masterpieces, but certainly not all of them. And while the rest shouldn't all be considered failures, there must have been quite a few that would not have received a passing grade from the artist or the public. And that's because failure is an essential part of the creative process.

We are all familiar with that clichéd image of writers at their desks, typing away before ripping the sheet of paper from the typewriter, balling it up and tossing it in a garbage can. (Sadly, the modern incarnation—a writer highlighting and deleting—just doesn't have the same dramatic flair.) But just because it is clichéd doesn't mean it isn't true. By their own reports, there are very few authors who do not rewrite and revise, and cut and expand their work, sometimes completely abandoning a project and starting something new. In a 1999 interview for the *Paris Review*, playwright Arthur Miller described his process like this: "I wish I had a routine for writing. I get up in the morning and I go out to my studio and I write. And then I tear it up! That's the routine, really. Then, occasionally, something sticks. And then I follow that."

Writers throw out work, painters abandon canvases and sculptors melt down sculptures. Often, however, the works are completed and sent out into the world, only to land with a heavy thud. Countless novels, songs, artworks and performances are quickly forgotten (some deservedly, others not). Sometimes, however, the failures live on in infamy. Writers and directors churn out enough bad films to make competition for the Razzie Awards (dubbed by *E! Online* as "the foremost authority on all things that suck on the big screen") as stiff as—heck, *more* stiff than—that for the Oscars.

Working creatively, trying to produce something that is new and unique, is hugely difficult. Of course, our efforts to be innovative are not always going to be successful. The November 16, 2014, edition of *New York Times Magazine*, the publication's "Innovation Issue," featured just one word on its cover: Failure. Its editorial introduction explained why: "A vast majority of innovative ideas fail, and most ingenious new products are just further iterations of previous flops. To truly love innovation, we must love failure."

Elon Musk knows the truth of that. Musk's entire career has been dedicated to innovation, of one sort or another. And from the beginning, he has been hushing the haters. Despite the fact that he had created two successful dotcom companies, including PayPal (which he sold to eBay for $1.5 billion in 2002), his other endeavours have been heckled repeatedly. In the early 2000s, he was on the receiving end of much derision for his plans to design and produce an electric sports car. (The skepticism was largely based on the fact that electric cars at the time were both anemic and awkward to maintain and run.) Likewise, his space program, SpaceX, raised the eyebrows and the laughter of techies and analysts alike.

And those waiting for Musk to fail were provided a number of opportunities for schadenfreude over the years.

The first Tesla cars were not hits and the company staggered in its early days, barely escaping bankruptcy after the financial crash of 2008. What's more, SpaceX experienced its own "failure to launch." Musk knew that he would probably have to make more than one attempt to get SpaceX airborne. He raised enough money for three launches. But his failure rate was even higher than he predicted. All three launches were a bust. He then had to scramble to find money for a fourth launch.

But that one did make it. As did the Tesla. A dozen years after he introduced his first electric car, the Model S Tesla sedan is a critical and commercial success. (It managed to score a total of 103 out of 100 on a *Consumer Reports* test, making the CR people scuttle back to their desks to revise their scoring system.) And its sales are rising steadily.

Apple, Microsoft and numerous wildly successful companies have experienced failure. Remember New Coke? Pepsi AM? How about Gerber Singles (jarred meals for adults)? Or Bic women's disposable underwear? (And of course there are myriad bad ideas that have *not* failed. How is it that aerosol cheese is still a thing?)

And this is because failure is part of creativity. Creativity is, after all, not an end product. It's a *process*. That can be a hard idea to really accept. So much of our lives—whether that's school or work—involves an evaluation of the end product. We are used to getting marks and performance reviews. We set goals and then track our progress on those goals—both individually and at the organizational level. In business, there's usually a host of analysts judging how our companies are doing in the market and evaluating every outcome.

But all this evaluation can be beside the point when we are attempting to think and work creatively—to innovate and create something new and worthwhile. Artists are well aware of this. As we discussed in Chapter 8, you can't focus on the negatives or second guess yourself constantly if you want to work creatively. Tina Fey said it best: "You can't be that kid standing at the top of the water slide, overthinking it. You have to go down the chute."

What's more, artists know that every bit of work, every effort that doesn't succeed, can eventually help them achieve success. Failure is how we refine, redirect and polish our ideas. It's how we learn. In his book on creativity, *The Mind's Best Work*, Harvard University professor of education D. N. Perkins labels this element of creative thinking "undoing":

> *Allowance has to be made for mistakes.... We have to be able to undo parts of the work and redo them, as well as undo plans that don't turn out well in favour of new plans. Such acts are the opposite of selection. They open up possibilities again, after we thought things were suitably narrowed down. At first thought, this seems only a regrettable consequence of human error, but not so. Often there is simply no reasonable way to detect difficulties other than by working through*

a situation until they appear. For instance, a mathematician may set out to prove a theorem that in fact is false. Only by attempting to prove it, failing, and searching long and hard for a counterexample can the mathematician finally discover that the mission is futile. Trial and error permeates human thought not just because people are less alert than they might be but because a trial selection often is the only way to give error a chance to show itself.

Indeed when it comes to failure, scientific discovery shares much of the same process as the arts. It's worth revisiting the words of John Maeda: "We know that the scientist's laboratory and the artist's studio are two of the last places reserved for open-ended inquiry, for *failure* to be a welcome part of the process, for learning to occur by a continuous feedback loop between thinking and doing." (Italics ours.)

British sculptor Polly Morgan would seem to agree. She advises aspiring artists to accept and appreciate the importance of their weakest work: "Don't wait for a good idea to come to you. Start by realising an average idea—no one has to see it. If I hadn't made the works I'm ashamed of, the ones I'm proud of wouldn't exist."

Elon Musk is another who acknowledges his failures have been a part of his companies' innovation strategies. In a 2003 email interview with HobbySpace.com, Musk lained, "Well, I have tried to learn as much as possible from prior attempts. If nothing else, we are committed to failing in a new way."

But perhaps the best known story about the importance of failure in the world of creativity and innovation is the invention of the Dyson vacuum. It all started when founder Sir James Dyson was cleaning up with a vacuum that was losing suction and he thought, "There must be a better way." There wasn't. So he invented it. In the process, he did away with vacuum bags and created his company's patented Cyclone Technology. He approached other vacuum manufacturers, willing to sell or license the technology. But most of these companies generated their profits not just from the appliance but also from the sale of bags. Who would invest in something that would eliminate a $500-million-a-year disposable bag business? Not them. They stayed focused on the old and familiar. Dyson decided to manufacture and sell his unique product on his own. Before long, Dyson was the number one vacuum in the United Kingdom.

But the really interesting part of Dyson's story is not the challenges he faced in the market. It's the challenges he faced in the lab. Dyson and his team built a staggering 5,126 prototypes before they got one that was good enough to bring to market. That means they "failed" 5,126 times! And it wasn't as if that process didn't create all sorts of difficulties for Dyson. In an article for *Wired* magazine, he wrote: "There are countless times an inventor can give up on an idea. By the time I made my 15th prototype, my third child was born. By 2,627, my wife and I were really counting our pennies. By 3,727, my wife was giving art lessons for some extra cash. These were tough times, but each failure brought me closer to solving the problem. It wasn't the final prototype that made the struggle worth it. The process bore the fruit. I just kept at it."

Dyson's patience and perseverance are to be lauded (and envied). But what we really love is that Dyson has been so open about the process and about the importance of failure. Writing in the *Globe and Mail*'s Leadership Lab column in August 2014, Dyson started this way: "Failure is such a taboo word. No one wants to be labelled a failure. No one wants to admit to it. And I just can't understand why." He explains that failure and learning from failure are an essential part of developing new technologies and approaches. Some lucky souls get it right the first time. But most innovation is the result a long and failure-filled development process. "I think the word 'failure' should be re-evaluated," he concludes. "It should be a term that is encouraged, accepted, even sought after. Because it's failure that drives invention forward."

Entrepreneur and musician David Usher also stresses the importance of failure: "So much of it is putting yourself out there. You have to be able to take a beating and go back out and have some more. That is the nature of making things. When you put stuff out into the world, that's the nature of business. You better have thick skin, take the beating, and learn from it."

If you want to be creative, if you want to make art, to innovate and to invent, you have to make moves that might fail. Refusing to do so will stop you before you even get started. As Ken Robinson has said, "If you're not prepared to be wrong, you'll never come up with anything original." But failure is *also* a powerful teaching tool that, if handled properly, can prevent larger, much more significant failure. Individuals and organizations that have never failed may not have the experience and the knowledge to make the best decisions. In other words, you need to fail small so you don't fail big. Take the sad story of Target Canada as a case in point.

Prior to Target's expansion into Canada in 2013, the company had been experiencing steady growth. Despite the recession and the gruelling retail environment post-2008, Target's revenue had increased year over year under the leadership of Gregg Steinhafel. So when the opportunity arose to buy the defunct Zellers chain's real estate and open well over a hundred stores in a brand-new market, Steinhafel put in a rich offer and prepared to reshape the Canadian retail landscape. But nothing went quite according to plan. Supply issues, checkout problems and a flawed inventory system made the initial three-store opening less than the shopping dream consumers were looking for—the openings of the rest of the stores were similar buzzkills for Canadians looking to recreate their cross-border purchasing frenzies.

Canadian Business writer Joe Castaldo noted that

"Steinhafel had joined Target in 1979, and his entire professional career had been spent with the company. Target experienced steady growth during that time, and Steinhafel had simply become accustomed to succeeding. 'The company had never really failed before,' says a former employee who worked in both the U.S. and Canada. There was no reason to think Target wouldn't be able to pull this off."

If Target, and Steinhafel, had experienced a few more setbacks as it expanded throughout the U.S., it might have been better able to predict the challenges it would face expanding in another country. If Steinhafel and other management had worked with other firms that had tried to broaden their international reach, they might have recognized the challenges of operating with different currencies, different import considerations and different retail competition. But Target had only experienced a more or less smooth road—it had no idea about the damage the Canadian potholes could do to its ride. In less than two years, Target Canada filed for bankruptcy.

But perhaps we are making failure sound as easy to endure as a day on the links. Failure—and the prospect of failure—can be downright terrifying. And denying that ugly fact is not helpful.

We tend to fling around many clichés when we give advice. You've heard them all before: "Follow your heart." "Hindsight is 20/20." "It ain't over till it's over." "Measure twice, cut once." And there's the one that's supposed to help us deal with the chance that things might not go according to plan. "What's the worst that can happen?" people say when the possibility of failure is making itself felt.

There's merit to a lot of the bromides, but the one that doesn't really bear close inspection is that last one, because anyone with a little imagination or even the slightest familiarity with the vagaries of life will be able to paint a pretty ugly picture of *the worst* in no time flat.

- "I'm thinking of leaving my seventeen-year-old at home for the weekend while we go out of town. *What's the worst that can happen?*" The worst that can happen is that news of the party goes viral, your place fills up with three hundred alcohol- and weed-fuelled kids, and you return home to a son in the slammer and a house that looks as if it went up against an earthquake and lost.

- "I don't know if I should quit my job to start my own business. *What's the worst that can happen?*" Your business could fail; you could be unable to find another job; you could lose your car, your house, and your credit rating. You could find your-self living in a cardboard box at forty-eight with your spouse, your three kids and your severely unimpressed cat.

- "Should I try the calamari? *What's the worst that can happen?*" You could have a severe gastro-intestinal reaction, which leaves you stuck in the facilities while the rest of your business team pitches your new project to senior management, who assume the guy who is now doing all the talking did all the work (which is so far from the truth that you want to scream), and that guy gets promoted to the fantastic position in Paris that you wanted, leaving you back at the home office, stewing and seething with resentment, which brings on more gastrointestinal difficulties, which makes your boss suggest that you might like to find a job better suited to your fragile constitution—and all because of a stupid plate of deep-fried calamari.

Identifying the worst thing that can happen is no way to overcome a fear of failure. If anything, it can amplify the fear to the point that you're running from the room shrieking in horror. (People who say, "What's the worst that can happen?" are usually the ones who have no vested interest in the situation that could be created if the worst *did* actually happen. And those are the people whose follow-up words of consolation will be, "Well, I didn't see *that* coming.")

Instead the best way to deal with a fear of failure is to refuse to bow to it—to either eliminate it from your psyche or find ways to contain it and push through it. As psychologist Maria Konnikova explains:

*Great thinkers have gotten over . . . the fear of
the void. Einstein had failures. So did Abraham
Lincoln, probably one of the few men to go to war
a captain and return a private—and to file for
bankruptcy before assuming the presidency. So
did Walt Disney, getting fired from a newspaper
for "lack of imagination" (the creativity paradox,
if ever there was one, in full force). So did Thomas
Edison, inventing over one thousand failed speci-
mens before he came up with the light bulb that
worked. . . . What distinguishes them isn't a lack
of failure but a lack of fear of failure, an openness
that is the hallmark of the creative mind.*

While many successful people seem not to be especially fearful types and many others have found ways to
get over their fears of failure, that may be cold comfort to
those of us who find ourselves more than a little reluctant
to face "the void," as Konnikova puts it. Sure, Abe Lincoln
and Thomas Edison weren't afraid, but they were Abe
Lincoln and Thomas Edison! (And to be frank, how do we
really know they weren't staring at the ceiling at three in
the morning thinking, *What have I gotten myself into?*)
But we don't necessarily have to be *unafraid.*

Fear of failure can be bad or it can be good. Bad fear
is the fear that you put in control. The fear that you allow
to make decisions for you. The fear that convinces you
to stop. (Just to be clear, we are talking creative efforts

here. If we are talking about walking on a barely frozen lake, or eating something from a dodgy-looking street cart, or running into zombies, fear is your friend. Listen to the fear.)

Good fear is the sort that signals you are actually doing something that is fresh and new and creative. We do seem to be hardwired to fear creativity—in others and in ourselves too. So feeling afraid may actually be a sign that you are onto something. David Bowie put it this way: "If you feel safe in the area you are working in, you're not working in the right area. Always go a little further into the water than you feel you're capable of being in. Go a little bit out of your depth. And when you don't feel your feet are quite touching the bottom, you're just about in the right place to do something exciting." Playwright Lucy Prebble says: "Feeling intimidated is a good sign. Writing from a place of safety produces stuff that is at best dull and at worst dishonest."

And even Silicon Valley entrepreneurs feel fear. Elon Musk has tried to debunk the myth that they don't. "I certainly have a fear of failure," he told an audience at the Dublin Web Summit in 2013. But he had this advice for handling that fear: "People should certainly ignore fear if it's irrational. Even if it's rational and the stake is worth it, it's still worth proceeding." At the same conference, Sherpa Ventures co-founder Shervin Pishevar also underlined the importance of accepting fear and the possibility of failure, yet moving ahead despite them: "Fear is finite, hope is infinite. We are afraid of failing, but it doesn't stop us from trying."

Indeed, most of us will need to accommodate some level of fear when facing a new endeavour—but we need to manage this emotion and push through it. Here actors and performers can show us the way. Many of our most respected actors, as well as other types of performers, spend their whole careers outside of their comfort zones. Stage fright afflicts a surprising number of accomplished thespians, and it can be much more than feeling slightly nervous. One study suggested that the stress of stage fright, which can result in shortness of breath, heart palpitations, blurred vision, vomiting and diarrhea, is the equivalent of the stress experienced in "a small car crash." Laurence Olivier was sometimes seized with stage fright to the point that he couldn't get onto the stage. Stephen Fry, Salma Hayek, Ian Holm, Bill Nighy, Sienna Miller, Keira Knightley and Hayden Panettiere have all talked openly about their struggles with stage fright. (Singers and musicians Barbra Streisand, Carly Simon, Adele, Brian Wilson, Cher, Andrea Bocelli and Glenn Gould have also suffered from severe stage fright.) Many actors say that they don't know a single actor who doesn't experience it from time to time. Some actors feel that if you aren't terrified every time you step on stage, you are probably not much of a performer.

And while occasionally actors do get sidelined by stage fright, most beat it back and perform anyway. They simply don't let it get in the way. Some even profess that the strong emotion gives them an adrenaline kick that fuels their performances.

One of the ways that we can keep fear of failure under wraps is to actually *experience* failure. In Chapter 8, we talked about the importance of confidence to creativity and in creative endeavours. Part of that essential confidence is the security of knowing that we can survive failures.

The idea that we must experience failure in order to build the confidence to grow, learn, take risks and achieve is gaining currency with educators and parents alike. The boomer generation and those who went before were raised by a society that felt that a little public humiliation was an excellent motivator. How else to explain that nasty 1960s practice of handing back tests to students in order of marks, wherein those with failing papers had to wait minute after excruciating minute for the ritual to be over? Or that of the fifties, when at least some local papers published the final grades of all gradu-ating high school students (not just the top marks, *all* of them)? With memories of red-lined essays and "who do you think you are?" pep talks, the boomer generation and their successors have embraced a parental and pedagog-ical culture of self-esteem building. Now, every child in little league gets a trophy for showing up and kindergar-ten "graduation" has become an hours-long awards cere-mony to name "top circle-time participant," "best guinea pig attendant" and "most consistent hand-washer."

The problem is that the pendulum has swung too far.

For one thing, kids aren't fooled. One dad we spoke to recently remembers his five-year-old son's tearful reaction to running a race at his school track and field day. "But you got a ribbon," the dad said, trying to avoid the meltdown. "It says five on it," said the boy. "I know what five means. Five means last." And he was right. Getting a ribbon didn't change the fact that the four other kids crossed the finish line ahead of him.

Not allowing children to fail sets them up to—well, if not to fail, at least not to succeed. As parent and teacher Jessica Lahey writes in her book *The Gift of Failure*, "Out of love and desire to protect our children's self-esteem, we have bulldozed every uncomfortable bump and obstacle out of their way, clearing the manicured path we hoped would lead to success and happiness. Unfortunately, in doing so we have deprived our children of the most important lessons of childhood. The setbacks, mistakes, miscalculations, and failures we have shoved out of our children's way are the very experiences that teach them how to be resourceful, persistent, innovative, and resilient citizens of this world."

When children fail, they may want to quit. But if they are encouraged to keep going, they learn to find new ways to do things, to expand their thinking and to problem solve. This trial and error approach helps us to realize that sometimes it takes much longer to master a skill than we would like to think. Acceptance of that fact is the basis of perseverance, resilience and strong work habits.

And perhaps most important, when parents and teachers allow children to fail while supporting them in their renewed efforts, they are letting the kids know that they have faith in their abilities to overcome challenges and to succeed on their own. They are helping children to put the fear of failure in its place. The resulting confidence that they can survive failure allows children to take risks—and taking risks is essential to continued learning, exploring and creating. (Remember fork, knife and butter?)

But those of us who long ago left the land of book reports and dodge ball can also find confidence by surviving failure. Stand-up comedian John Mulaney knows all about that. Interviewed for CBC Radio's *Q* in November 2015, Mulaney was asked to talk about his recently cancelled TV show *Mulaney*. It could have been a touchy interview. Until that show, Mulaney's career had seemed pretty golden: a long stint as a staff writer at *Saturday Night Live* and series of wildly successful stand-up engagements. Based on his growing popularity, Fox Network asked him to create, write and star in a sitcom. And that he did.

The resulting comedy, *Mulaney*, was, by all accounts, a Hindenburg of a TV show. Fox cancelled it almost immediately (although it did continue to air all thirteen painful episodes that had been filmed). The failure of his eponymous show did not, however, shake Mulaney's faith in himself or his work. On the contrary: he says that there was "something interesting about [seeing] a project with my name on it crash into a wall. Almost exhilarating. Almost the same kind of thing as when [you have success]." Part of that exhilaration was what he discovered about his ability to handle failure. "This is fine, this is survivable," he remembers thinking. And he was comforted by what Lorne Michaels had told him: "This is what showbiz is. You fail 98 per cent and if you succeed 2 per cent of the time, it's huge." That knowledge, that failure was an inevitable part of the work he was doing and that he could manage it, gave him the confidence to hit the road with a brand-new stand-up routine just six months after filming the final episode of *Mulaney*. And the new show was a testament to John's renewed sense of self. It was called *The Comeback Kid*.

Peter Aceto, the president and CEO of Tangerine (formerly ING), has a slightly different take on failure and confidence. He suggests, "Let mistakes happen. Be comfortable with the mistakes, because failure is an important lesson. It helps modify and adjust ideas and reassess objectives. But don't fail too often, because you risk losing your confidence. Simplify the strategy as much as possible. Involve more people early. Make incremental changes."

Peter Aceto's warning not to fail too often is understandable, but if we are really paying attention to why and how we have failed, it may not be necessary. Learning from our mistakes makes us far less likely to repeat them—the power of failure to teach is what makes it a truly useful experience. (That said, it can be challenging for large organizations to retain what they've learned from failure. In his interesting *Harvard Business Review* article, entitled

"Why Organizations Forget What They Learn from Failures," Francisco Polidoro, Jr., associate professor at the McCombs School of Business at the University of Texas at Austin, explains how the pressures to find efficiencies and launch new products, along with executive turnover, often lead corporations to neglect the valuable insights they receive from failed efforts.)

We have argued that people need to be able to accept some failure as part of the personal creative process. But tolerating failure needs to be something that you do for others as well as for yourself. If you are in a leadership position, you need to create environments that support a trial and error approach—that is, to allow others to fail if you want the people in our families and our workplaces to be creative thinkers, problem solvers, innovators or inventors. Film director Ian Rickson advises artists who work with others to "try to create an atmosphere where people feel free to take risks. Fear can shut down creativity, as can the pressure to impress."

The Lean Startup's CEO Eric Ries, in his *Harvard Business Review* essay "Become a Company that Questions Everything," notes that part of the creation of a corporate culture that encourages curiosity, problem solving and innovation is the allowance for failure. "It's not about slogans or putting up posters on the wall—it's about the systems and the incentives you create to promote the behavior," he writes. He goes on to point out that at most companies, "the resources flow to the person with the most confident, best plan. Or the person with no failures on their record." But he argues that companies need to direct more budgetary resources to those who are exploring unanswered questions, conducting promising experiments, and taking intelligent risks. If you are not doing this, your company is not going to be making the kind of breakthroughs that spell success.

Elon Musk is even more blunt and more succinct about the need to encourage risk taking: "Failure is an option here," he says of his companies. "If things are not failing, you're not innovating enough."

And finally, another reason why taking risks and allowing ourselves to fail is so important to success is that in our flops, we may very well find hidden gold. Take Post-it notes. Post-it notes were developed by 3M innovator Arthur Fry after he heard about a "failed" product development by another 3M scientist, Dr. Spencer Silver. Silver had been attempting to develop a new adhesive but had, in the end, produced a substance that was only slightly tacky. Silver had been casting about for a use for the stuff, which he had dubbed "a solution without a problem." It was Fry who saw the treasure in a glue that didn't quite do what it was supposed to do.

Further back in history is the inadvertent creation of the modern eraser. Before the late eighteenth century, people used little balls of moistened bread to erase graphite pencil marks. Then in about 1770, English optician and scientific-instrument maker Edward Nairne reached for a remnant of bread but picked up a piece of natural rubber instead. The rubber worked perfectly on the pencil marks. He began selling his rubber erasers a short time later. (There is, however, a little confusion about his discovery; about the same time, philosopher and inventor Joseph Priestley also wrote about the erasing properties of rubber.) And more recently, a drug that failed to treat angina was nevertheless an enormous financial success. Although a bust for relieving the feeling of pressure and the spasms of the coronary arteries and the heart muscle, it did have a surprising side effect. Not one that anyone would want to deal with if they were suffering stabbing chest pain mind you, but one men might actually enjoy if they were feeling a little better. The developers did a 180, and Viagra hit the shelves a few years later.

In any new, exciting creative endeavour, some element of failure is almost inevitable. But let's follow the artists and the innovators and embrace the power of failure. By seeing its potential to teach, by acknowledging that our mistakes help us improve our ideas, by pushing past our fear of being wrong, we will be able to make discoveries, explore possibilities and achieve something new, different and worthwhile.

Just remember, if you are working creatively, you're going to fail. And when you do, success will be following right behind you.

" *Art is a human activity, consisting in this, that one man consciously, by means of certain external signs, hands on to others feelings he has lived through, and that other people are infected by these feelings and also experience them.*"

—Leo Tolstoy

ALWAYS CONNECT

Over the course of this book, we have looked at how artists do what they do, and we've talked about how embracing these practices and attitudes can help us all to think and act more creatively. We have argued that everyone has the stuff it takes to be an artist, even if the last thing they painted was the bathroom walls and their attempts at singing have led to the cancellation of the office karaoke nights.

There is still one more lesson that art and artists can teach us about innate creativity and about being more effective in almost every avenue of life. And it is perhaps the most powerful tool we have for making the most of our work, social and family lives. It's our ability to connect with others.

One of our friends poses an unusual question every time she considers which movie to see or TV show to watch: "How much am I going to cry during that?" She voices frustration with sites like Rotten Tomatoes and RogerEbert.com that simply use a "like or dislike" rating system. She'd like a zero-to-ten Kleenex scale as well. She doesn't necessarily avoid the movies that are going to make her weep; she just wants to make sure that she is physically up for a possible crying jag—and that she is prepared with waterproof mascara and an adequate tissue supply.

There's nothing startling in the observation that some movies, books and music have the power to make mascara run and nasal passages congest. But it's interesting to note that *all* art, even something as inert as a two-tonne steel sculpture, can elicit powerful emotions from viewers. It's easy to explain heartfelt responses to paintings and sculptures with religious or socially sensitive content. Renditions of the *Pietà* are particularly poignant for Christians. Even during the painter's own time, Jean-François Millet's portraits of poor farm labourers played upon the viewer's sympathy for people whose lives were back-breaking work. But how to explain the tears evoked by less "narrative" art, like the entirely abstract paintings of Mark Rothko? Rothko's canvases—consisting of almost monochromatic colour—are apparently some of the most cried-over works by a modern artist. The Rothko Chapel in Houston, a non-denominational centre, is dubbed on its website as "a stillness that moves." Its walls display fourteen large dark canvases with subtle washes of colour that are said to provoke existential thoughts of mortality, spirituality, transcendence and self-reflection. It's a popular spot for meditation. And its guest book is a log of misty-eyed reactions (and, we imagine, the occasional "I just don't get it"). That Rothko's huge abstract paintings evoke such emotion and psychological tumult is testimony to the power of art and artists to connect with people.

Many argue that the emotional responses we feel are actually what makes art ... well, art. A study conducted by psychologists Gerald C. Cupchik, Oshin Vartanian, Adrian Crawley and David J. Mikulis, from the University of Toronto and York University, used functional MRI to study the brains of people observing works of art versus ordinary objects. When people were looking at artworks, the parts of their brain linked with emotional responses—and with goal setting—were active. When the subjects looked at other sorts of objects, these parts of the brain were quiet. The researchers noted that certain things, like symmetry and open landscapes (which have connections, in an evolutionary sense, to the business of survival), produce feelings of serenity or assurance. Darkness and unclear scenes provoke fear. And artworks that may be initially puzzling or obscure to viewers make us want to figure them out (the goal-setting response). When we find meaning or pattern, we are flooded with feelings of satisfaction. Because art involves the participation of viewer, listener or reader, some psychologists have argued that it is the most powerful form of emotional communication that we have.

It may sound like the pronouncement of Captain Obvious (to borrow from a recent ad campaign) to say that artists have an extraordinary ability to connect with people. And yet, as we discussed earlier in Chapter 5 and in Chapter 7, when artists are in the midst of creating, they are usually trying foremost to satisfy themselves, to work out puzzles and answer questions for themselves. They are less likely to be thinking about the connections they might make through the canvas they are working on or the notes they are stringing together. They may not be conscious of their audience at all.

During the 1940s, a school of literary criticism, dubbed "New Criticism," argued that an author was not always fully aware of what he or she was creating, and that when looking for meaning in a poem or a novel, the reader should not consider the author's intention or even try to decipher what that might have been. Readers, they felt, were the ones who created the meaning in a piece of art— it was the interaction between the reader and the work that was important. In other words, the author's intent had little to do with the meaning of or the success of a piece of art. To think otherwise was to fall prey to what these critics labelled the "intentional fallacy."

Yet art *is* expression, and it's almost impossible to imagine musicians, writers, actors or playwrights working without the hope of an audience. If that were not so,

Picasso, van Gogh and every other painter would have simply painted over their work when they were no longer interested in staring at it. (You may be thinking that artists try to share their work because they need to sell it in order to make money to survive. But that doesn't explain why artists who have achieved financial security continue to display their work, or why writers, musicians and sculptors who make money from other sorts of labour—their "day jobs"—still send their art out into the world.) It seems fair to argue that artists connect, both intentionally *and* unconsciously.

So how do artists connect with their audiences so strongly—and what can the rest of us learn from them? Art, we would argue, communicates so powerfully with people because it conveys a deep understanding of the human condition.

Certain kinds of artists put themselves in others' shoes in order to create. Novelists and actors are probably the most obvious examples. As actor Tom Hiddleston says, "Actors in any capacity, artists of any stripe, are inspired by their curiosity, by their desire to explore all quarters of life, in light and in dark, and reflect what they find in their work. Artists instinctively want to reflect humanity, their own and each other's, in all its intermittent virtue and vitality, frailty and fallibility."

Great artists do this so well that their work makes us understand how others think and feel. A number of recent studies have shown that reading fiction, which often takes us into the lives and minds of others in an intense way, can make people more empathetic. After finishing a good book, we may feel as if we know what it is like to be an escaped slave in the antebellum South or a coal miner in Victorian England. But literature can also help us imagine what might be going through the mind of our reclusive neighbour or the grumpy grocery store clerk.

But while art may come from a kind of empathetic under-standing and may encourage empathy in others, artists are not always empathetic toward others, as the biographies of many make clear. They may be self-absorbed, selfish, antisocial or insensitive to those around them. (We can't help thinking about Ernest Hemingway suggesting to his first wife that she invite his lover into the household, just to make it more merry. Or Frank Lloyd Wright's rigid refusal to let his wife have the fresh-cut flowers that she so loved in their architecturally pristine home.) Yet it would seem that almost all great artists are deeply in tune with some essential aspects of the human condition, even if they themselves are empathetic in only an imaginative, abstract way.

What does this mean for creativity and our own creative work? We would argue that conscious manipulation—trying to figure out what people want, what they will react positively to, what will have meaning—is not enough to connect with people. Coming from a place of empathy and understanding of others, and responding authenti-cally to ideas that excite us or that we feel passionately about, are more likely to make connections. (As Steve Jobs's famous line goes, "A lot of times, people don't know what they want until you show it to them.") In other words, as we mentioned in our discussion of the importance of authenticity in the Introduction and elsewhere, we need to believe in what we are doing in order to connect with people, as artists do.

When we are trying to work creatively, when we are struggling to innovate, empathy can be a powerful tool. Using our imaginations to put ourselves in others' shoes, *truly* seeing the world from the perspective of others and understanding human responses, allows us to produce solutions, ideas or works that connect with people. In a 2001 interview with *USA Today*, Michael Eisner, the former CEO of the Walt Disney Company, credited his degree in literature and theatre with helping him success-fully navigate the corporate world: "Literature is unbeliev-ably helpful, because no matter what business you are in, you are dealing with interpersonal relationships. It gives you an appreciation of what makes people tick."

Empathy can help us understand what products our customers want or might want (like James Dyson with his innovative vacuum cleaner or Biz Stone with Twitter). It can let us see which health care solutions might work for our patients. It can allow us to teach and share informa-tion in a way that makes sense to our staff.

If you don't feel that you are naturally empathetic or that your innate empathy isn't quite up to snuff, you can work to improve it. (If "what the hell are they thinking?" is your constant refrain, you might need an empathy tune-up. Either that or you're at Comic-Con.) Quieting the mind and focusing inward is a time-honoured way of making a deeper connection with our own emotions and natures. Meditation is a good tool for working on empathy.

Understanding ourselves is key to being able to understand the emotional lives of others. Taking a moment to figure out how we are feeling and why we are feeling this way is something many of us rarely do. But getting in the habit of checking in on our emotional state can not only be helpful in our own lives, it can also help us deal more sensitively and effectively with others. (For example, if you have figured out that last time you were impatient with your son, it was because you were actually nervous about the mountain bike path he wanted to ride with you, you may be more likely to recognize that your business partner is resisting your suggestions because he's anxious the project is beyond his abilities.)

Careful listening to and watching those around you can also help you to decode other people's attitudes and biases and to adopt their point of view. The next time you are on the subway or at a cocktail party, take some time to be an observer instead of an active player. Pay attention to body language and to really hearing what people are saying. See if you can read between the lines of a conversation and imagine what is going on in people's minds as they speak.

Group therapy, marriage counselling and team-building sessions are all big on role-playing games. And for good reason. This imaginative adoption of another's point of view is a great way to build empathy, and it doesn't have to be a public performance. Even if you are the sort who winces at the thought of participating in a skit at your corporate professional development weekend, you can quietly use the technique on your own. Try to imagine what your co-worker will feel about your suggestion for a new business strategy—before you settle on how you are going to present that strategy. Try to imagine what it is like to be your fifteen-year-old daughter before you plan that family holiday.

And of course, perhaps the easiest and most painless way to improve your empathy—read some good fiction!

Empathy is the key to truly connecting with people, but it is a subtle skill—and as we have said, one not always associated with the personalities of artists. But there is one way that we can all connect, one art form that is always at our fingertips, and that is through storytelling.

Storytelling is, after all, the one creative activity that we all engage in—even if we're not aware of it most of the time. Psychologists and pedagogical experts have argued that the way in which we think and learn is based on stories. Unlike computers, humans have a hard time processing and remembering discrete pieces of information or links between facts. In order to retain information and relation-ships, we create stories that help us hold on to material.

Storytelling, in other words, is essential to memory and to understanding.

Michael Gazzaniga, cognitive neuroscientist and director of the SAGE Center for the Study of the Mind at University of California Santa Barbara, has been studying storytelling and the brain for years. But he is also one of the neuroscientists who first showed that the left and right lobes of the brain carried out different cognitive functions. While his initial experiments established that the left lobe controlled things such as language, logic and analysis, and the right lobe was the home of imagination, intuition and feelings, later experiments with subjects in whom the communication between the lobes was absent (because of injury or surgery) revealed interesting aspects of how we think and learn.

Gazzaniga was able to show that when a split-brain subject was presented with something that didn't make sense, areas in the left lobe (which he dubbed "the interpreter") kicked in. As you may remember, the left lobe controls the right side of the body and vice versa. So Gazzaniga and his researchers were able to give directions to one side of the brain or the other by allowing only the left or the right eye to read instructions. What they noticed was that if the researchers gave a direction to the right hemisphere to do something, it would make the left hand follow those directions. But the right side of the brain is non-verbal. So when Dr. Gazzaniga asked the patient why his left hand had done what it had done, the answer had to come from the left lobe, which—because of the lack of communication between the two lobes—had no idea why his hand had just drawn a circle or tapped on the table.

But that is not what the patients would say. Instead, they would create a story to explain what they had done. A 2011 *New York Times* profile of Dr. Gazzaniga described one of his experiments in which the left hemisphere was shown a picture of a chicken claw and the right was shown a picture of snow. Then both hemispheres were shown a series of pictures and the subject was asked to pick two drawings to go with the previous pictures he had seen. He picked a chicken and a shovel. When he was asked to explain his choices, he was able to describe the association between the left-lobe pictures: the chicken went with the claw. But the right hemisphere, while it clearly associated the snow and the shovel, couldn't communicate that to the language centre on the left. So the left hemisphere, which hadn't seen the snow, concocted a logical explanation. The man explained that you would need a shovel to clean up after a chicken (the fellow clearly had some farming background!).

What is particularly fascinating is that "the interpreter" seems to be a left-brain function—a function of our ability to analyze and make sense of the world (not part of our "imaginative" right brain). In other words, storytelling is a basic processing function of the brain—a way we take information and make sense of it by connecting the dots, often with guesses and assumptions. Our left-brain abilities, our imaginations, it would seem, can raise those stories to artistic and literary greatness.

Why is this so important? First, it shows that both the left and right lobes are involved in the act of creating. And that even logical left-brain thinkers are accessing a sort of creativity as they think about the world. (It's also a good reminder that our understanding is largely subjective. Our brains try to impose logic and order on things, even when it's not there!) But more importantly, perhaps, is that because storytelling is how we understand the world, it is also the best way to make ourselves understood. If we tell our stories, and allow ourselves to think in terms of stories, we are much more likely to get our message across.

Almost every kind of art is storytelling in some way or other. Song lyrics are often narratives, but music alone can tell a tale (think of Vivaldi's *Four Seasons* or Aaron Copeland's *Billy the Kid*). And we surely don't have to tell you that paintings are worth a thousand words (and that sometimes clichés are true).

Outside of the art world, certain businesses and disciplines have long relied on great narratives to get results. Storytelling has always been a technique in creating memorable, effective advertising. And if the gazillion episodes of *Law and Order* are to be believed, good storytelling is essential to winning a court case. Paul Smith, consumer research executive, corporate trainer and author of *Lead with a Story: A Guide to Crafting Business Narratives that Captivate, Convince, and Inspire*, has identified twenty-one common business and life challenges in which storytelling is helpful. Among them are leading change, establishing a company vision, giving feedback, managing inclusion and diversity, conveying what you believe in, defining values and teaching. In an interview with *Forbes* magazine, Smith notes that many of the corporate big hitters like Microsoft, Berkshire Hathaway, Saatchi & Saatchi, Procter & Gamble, NASA, the World Bank and Kimberly Clark include storytelling as a business strategy or provide storytelling instruction during their executive training. He notes that "3M banned bullet points and replaced them with a process of writing 'strategic narratives.' P&G has hired Hollywood movie directors to teach its senior executives how to lead better with storytelling. And some of the storytellers at Motorola belong to outside improvisational or theater groups to hone their story skills."

And it's not just the business world that has begun to appreciate the value of a good tale. A Penn State College of Medicine study found that medical students who had been told the life stories of dementia patients found it easier to treat these patients than students who hadn't. Storytelling also significantly improved the adherence to treatment for hypertension patients, according to a study by the University of Massachusetts Medical School.

One of the publishing people we met during the writing of this book related how telling a story helped her solve a business problem. She was trying to get approval for a book acquisition she wanted to make. She had run all of the numbers, but when she saw the results of the P&L,

she knew that the maximum offer that the calculations produced was unlikely to win her the project. It was the exact same amount that she had offered for the author's last book, and while it was fair, she knew that the author would see it as an insult—a demotion almost. The unimproved advance would suggest that in the intervening three years, despite having another critically acclaimed book under his belt, his worth to the publisher had not grown, that the publisher didn't expect increased success with the new book. And she knew that he was being wooed by other houses. Even if another publisher didn't offer more money, he might decide that it was worth being the bright, fresh star at a new publisher instead of the solid but underestimated veteran at the old one.

To be able to offer more money than the P&L allowed, the editor needed to get approval from her CFO. When she sat down with him, the CFO immediately started thumbing through the P&L. He adjusted a few numbers, but was shaking his head. It didn't make sense, he said, to offer any more money. If the new book's sales numbers dropped, the modest advance would mean that the bottom line would not be hit as hard if the larger advance was not earned out. And if the book did better than expected, the author would get additional income from the royalties as the sales mounted up. Besides, the amount of the proposed increase was so small, he didn't see how it would significantly change the financial situation of the author.

It was clear to the editor that the numbers simply couldn't capture the reality of the situation, so she took the P&L back and asked the CFO if she could tell him a story. She began by explaining how the author had come to the publisher in the first place and how their relationship had evolved over the years. Then she told him about the author's other jobs, his relationship with other publishers and his home life. Finally, she talked about how he saw his future and what his aspirations were. In short, she tried to create a mini-bio and hoped that the CFO would begin to see the world through the author's eyes and would realize why even a small gesture of confidence would be so important to him. It worked. She got approval for the better offer and got the book.

Of course, the success of any negotiation or transaction is often dependent on the ability of the parties to stand in each other's shoes. And the fastest way to allow people to do this is by sharing stories. You can probably think of dozens of times that telling stories has helped you to make yourself understood, convince someone, or change an opponent's mind. But we are often reticent to employ storytelling in our career or business lives. We shouldn't be. Storytelling is a great tool to teach or to persuade, but it is also a way we can stretch our creative muscle in our working lives. We may not be able to paint a picture or write a symphony (or at least we can't do those things while leading a board meeting). But we all have stories that we can tell. That said, some people are better storytellers than others. If you're one of those people who always seem to lead with the punchline, don't despair: creating great narratives is a skill that can be developed with practice.

When we listen to our speakers at The Art Of events, we notice that many of our guests are masters at storytelling. And those engaging stories all seem to use the same patterns and techniques. They are dependent on rising and falling tension, and that tension is created by raising questions in the listener's mind—what will happen? where is this going?—and by the gradual revelation of information. As you may remember from your high school English class, this is the *arc* of the story. The tension rises until there is a turning point (a crisis or climax in English-class lingo), at which point it falls away and the story reaches some kind of conclusion. The best stories usually have small twists or little surprises along the way, and our favourites have a few laughs too.

If you can't, like the P&G execs, get Hollywood directors to help you hone your skills (you could invite Steven Spielberg to drop by the office, but we hear he's quite busy), you can follow the Motorola execs' lead and take a few improv or writing classes. But the easiest way to improve your storytelling skills is to pay attention to the good stories you hear and think a little about why you enjoyed them. Then you can try to employ a few of the techniques yourself. (At The Art Of, we also like to collect good stories from others and retell them. Good artists borrow. Great artist steal.) It's interesting to note that while creative writing courses are springing up everywhere like literary Tim Hortons, many writers feel that the only value of these programs is to make students do the assignments. In other words, the best way to learn how to write is to write. The best way to become a better storyteller is to tell stories. Just get 'er done.

You may have been skeptical about the assertion expressed in the title of this book: Everyone is an artist. Our ability to tell stories is one way in which this is undeniably true.

IN TODAY'S WORLD, IT seems that more and more people are recognizing the extraordinary things that can happen when the arts cross-pollinate with other disciplines, when we tap into our creative selves and harness our intrinsic artistic abilities. A growing number of organizations are popping up to facilitate these efforts. The Rhode Island School of Design's work with the scientific community was mentioned earlier. The University of Guelph is also home to a wonderful cross-disciplinary institute. Born of the Guelph's Jazz Festival and the university's music department, the International Institute for Critical Studies in Improvisation (IICSI) focuses on the powerful creative tools used in improvisational jazz to develop social policies and programs. The program's founder, Dr. Ajay Heble, notes on the institute's website that IICSI works with five other universities, thirty community-based organizations and fifty-eight researchers from twenty different institutions, including health care centres and government agencies, to create "positive social change through the confluence of improvisational arts, innovative scholarship, and collaborative action." But learning to work like jazz musicians do—by improvising within an existing framework—is clearly key.

And it's the reason Dr. John Semple, whom we met in the Introduction, has become involved in the program. "I am looking at jazz as a model of improvisation to help map where your thinking processes go when you leave structure behind." In particular, he is investigating how jazz-inspired improvisation can help surgeons deal with unanticipated events that force them to modify routine procedures. Dr. Heble's description of the research project ("Improvisation, Community and Social Practice") that was the beginning of IICSI makes it clear that musical improvisation does indeed demand the same kinds of skills that surgeons need in an unexpected crisis: shared responsibility and "an ability to negotiate differences . . . a willingness to accept the challenges of risk and contingency."

These are abilities that help people work collaboratively and creatively in any area, so it's not surprising that the business world has embraced improvisation too. Take McGill University's Faculty of Management. When MBA students show up for Assistant Professor Suzanne Gagnon's organizational behaviour class, they may be in for a surprise. Instead of sitting through a Power-

Point presentation or a lecture, they might find themselves taking the stage, improvising a scene with another classmate or engaging in a performance exercise. That's because Professor Gagnon regularly invites actor and improv coach Rob Nickerson to lead sessions with her business students. It's part of her approach to teaching collaboration and leadership skills. Indeed, Gagnon and Nickerson are the co-authors of an academic paper entitled "Learning to Lead, Unscripted: Developing Affiliative Leadership Through Improvisational Theatre." In a *Globe and Mail* profile of Nickerson and his improv work with McGill, the actor observes, "A lot of people are linear thinkers, so to have this part of people's brains open up is like discovering you own 10 acres of land instead of five." We can't think of a better metaphor to describe the value of letting our creative selves flourish.

Yes, Fortune 500 companies are hiring Hollywood directors to teach executives; business schools are using acting coaches; CEOs are searching out liberal arts grads for their businesses; and scientific communities are hooking up with design schools. Throughout the business, science and technology worlds, the value of artistic abilities and sensibilities is increasingly recognized. The twenty-first century seems to be welcoming the Renaissance man (and woman) like never before (or at least like never since the actual Renaissance).

And, as we hope we have shown, there is plenty of evidence to explain why. If you need just a little more convincing, consider this: a recent article in the *New York Times* about how to raise a creative child noted that many winners of the Nobel Prizes for science tend to have one thing in common. They have a wide range of interests that often include the arts: "Relative to typical scientists, Nobel Prize winners are 22 times more likely to perform as actors, dancers or magicians; 12 times more likely to write poetry, plays or novels; seven times more likely to dabble in arts and crafts; and twice as likely to play an instrument or compose music."

The statistic may be surprising at first, but we shouldn't be any more taken aback than if we were told that hockey players tend to be good golfers. When we exercise our creative powers in one area, we are much more likely to be able to use that creative muscle in another discipline. But the habits and attitudes that making art encourages also help us think and act more creatively. When we are artists, we reinvent ourselves and are a little unrealistic. We ask questions, and we stop, look and listen. We move past competition and hush the haters. When we are artists, we get 'er done, and we flip our flops. And finally, when we are artists, we genuinely and profoundly connect with people.

Go and make interesting mistakes, make amazing mistakes, make glorious and fantastic mistakes. Break rules. Leave the world more interesting for your being here. Make. Good. Art."

—Neil Gaiman, author

ACKNOWLEDGEMENTS

Many of you reading this book are neck deep in responsibilities, scrambling to prepare for the next business day and probably squeezing in some quality time to expand your intellectual horizons. You're super busy and we'd like to acknowledge your commitment to the written word. You could be binge-watching Netflix, but you've chosen to read this book. Thanks for the trust.

We're also a little busy. Between running companies, speaking and travelling, we're on the road a lot and we couldn't do what we do without the support of some pretty special people.

Our teams: The dedicated professionals at The Tite Group and The Art Of diligently help run our businesses while we, the faces of the organizations, often get the attention, press and books. We know that writing about what to do is far easier than actually doing it.

Our publisher: Brad Wilson, Rob Firing, Meg Masters and the entire team at HarperCollins have been entrepreneurial in approach, passionate about the topic and patient with the process. Who's coming on the book tour?

Our friends: Whether they've graced the stages at The Art Of events around North America or populated discussions on Speak and Spill Mastermind, there are speakers all over the world who have inspired, educated, humoured and supported us. You know who you are. And we don't have time for a Q & A.

Our families: Our wives and children (well, Scott's children) have supported this initiative and all the activities that inspired it from the very beginning. Christy, Rachel and Emily, you somehow manage to support our work while successfully pursuing your own. Where do you find the time? We'll be home by seven. Maybe seven thirty.

TAG. YOU'RE IT.

Now that you've read the book, you'll probably want to rush out and start applying all the principles we've covered. Obviously, we don't expect (or want) readers to go out and start painting, sculpting, or breaking into random interpretive dances on public transportation. It's not about actually being an artist. It's about integrating the beliefs and behaviours of artists to improve other aspects of your life. Creativity can help you become a better marketer, salesperson, accountant, spouse, parent, neighbour, community citizen, or any other role you play on a daily basis.

We're really excited to see what you'll do. Make us proud. When you're at your creative best, let us know! Just share whatever it is you've done on #IamAnArtist. For continued inspiration, head on over to EveryonesAnArtist.ca.

Think like an artist. Act like an artist. Inspire and be inspired.

Start now.